seema's SHOW

a volume
in the
counterculture
series

Editors: David Farber, History, Temple University
Beth L. Bailey, American Studies, Temple University

Series

seema's SHOW
a Life on the Left

SARA HALPRIN

FOREWORD BY MARGE FRANTZ

UNIVERSITY OF NEW MEXICO PRESS | ALBUQUERQUE

10 09 08 07 06 05   1 2 3 4 5 6

Library of Congress Cataloging-in-Publication Data

Halprin, Sara.
  Seema's show : a life on the left / Sara Halprin ;
foreword by Marge Frantz.—1st ed.
      p. cm. — (CounterCulture series)
  Includes bibliographical references and index.
  ISBN 0-8263-3847-x (pbk. : alk. paper)
  1. Weatherwax, Seema, 1905–   2. Women political activists—United States—
Biography.   3. Women photographers—United States—Biography.
4. Russian Americans—Biography.   5. Counterculture—United States.
I. Title.   II. Series.

CT275.W3494H35 2005
979.4'0049171'0092—dc22

2005006821

Two lines from "Red-nosed Frost" ("Moroz Drasnyy Nos") from *Nikolai Nekrasov: Poems, 1862–1863*, by Nikolai Nekrasov, edited by Juliet Soskice, translator (1936). By permission of Oxford University Press.

Design and composition: Melissa Tandysh

It is very important to be stubborn
when you are losing your independence.

—Seema Aissen Weatherwax

contents

List of photographs

foreword

The prospect of an afternoon with Seema Weatherwax lights up one's life. A visit over a few cups of tea with this fascinating woman of ninety-nine years instructs and delights. And now, happily, her story is available to more than those who are fortunate to be in her circle. Prepare to enjoy!

Seema's story is not only enjoyable, it's instructive and important. The years of the Cold War and McCarthyism left their ugly stains on many Americans' understanding of leftists like Seema. But here's a fresh and welcome look at a small part of that world—which helps overcome that distorted segment of our history.

Among many other insights, you get a close-up view of how one dissident went about her life. In the twenty-first century, it may be difficult for younger readers, especially, to imagine why people joined the communist movement in such numbers in the 1930s and 1940s, with such enthusiasm and dedication. Here, you see Seema, who had been a leftist since the 1920s, bringing people of all races together at every opportunity, creating those opportunities, leading in efforts for racial and economic justice. Far from the brainwashed caricatures of the movement so often portrayed, Seema emerges as a sharp, indefatigable, and valuable player in the life of her time.

From her participation in the Left-led Film and Photo League, the support of loyalists in the Spanish Civil War, the birth of the United Nations, the struggle against blacklisting during the McCarthy years, to the early women's movement, Seema was part and parcel of the struggles of her day. Despite FBI harassment, she never slowed down.

I first met Seema and became one of her many admirers when she moved to Santa Cruz in her early eighties. She very soon became a leading light in the local branches of the Women's International League for Peace and Freedom (in which I was active) and the National Association for the Advancement of Colored People.

I soon learned about her career as an outstanding photographic printer and her work with Ansel Adams in Yosemite, and how her life had touched other leading photographers of her time—Edward Weston, Imogen Cunningham, and Dorothea Lange, among others—as well as old left icons like Woody Guthrie, and I also remembered the novel of her sister-in-law Clara Weatherwax. I was thrilled to see Seema's own extraordinary photographic exhibitions later on.

I believe Seema would agree with me that her generation of women in the old left was a profoundly fortunate generation. We were part of a movement for social justice, economic justice, and racial justice that made our lives rich and fulfilling. We enjoyed a community of comrades close beyond compare, and you will meet many of them in this book. We lived fully and creatively. We were assaulted by the full power of American capitalism, but the community survived and the struggle for justice continues in newer forms.

I am grateful that Sara Halprin has made this intriguing combination of oral history, memoir, and biography come to life for a larger audience.

Marge Frantz

Santa Cruz, California

2004

figure 1. Seema Weatherwax, Yosemite, photograph by Edward Weston, 1940. Courtesy of Special Collections, University Library, University of California, Santa Cruz. Seema Weatherwax Collection. ©1981 Center for Creative Photography, Arizona Board of Regents.

INtRODUCtION

*I've always seen my political work as building connections
instead of tearing down oppressive systems.*

—Seema

a Life woRtH LiviNG

At seventy-nine, when her husband Jack died, Seema had already
lived a rich life, spanning three continents, intimately connected with
the American left and the progressive counterculture of the early and
middle twentieth century. She was close to well-known figures in art
and music, especially Ansel Adams, for whom she worked as darkroom
assistant in Yosemite. She had been a political activist since the age of
nineteen, when she joined the Young Communist League in Boston.
Seema and Jack had formed and maintained close connections with
the African-American community where they lived for years in Los
Angeles, with the Philippine family to whom they became adoptive
grandparents, with many friends and a large extended family. They had
organized countless events, from family celebrations to benefit concerts
and political demonstrations, and now Jack was gone.

This was to be their golden time. Three weeks earlier, after forty-
four hectic years of married life in Los Angeles, they had moved to

Santa Cruz, where Seema hoped they would have time to walk together by the little stream near their garden apartment and listen to the birds.

Instead, she lay in bed alone at night, listening to herself moan as if it were someone else crying.

I just talked to myself. I said, "Am I going to sit back, or can I do something to make life worthwhile?"

Making life worthwhile, for Seema, meant contributing to the political, social, and cultural life of her community. That was how she had been raised. As a five-year-old in her parents' home in Russia she stood in front of company and recited a poem by Nekrasov, one of Lenin's favorite poets.

By the time I met her, fourteen months after Jack's death, Seema was already an active member of several progressive groups in Santa Cruz, and she had begun to make new friends in her new home while maintaining contact with the old. She introduced herself to me on my answering machine, calling to comment on one of my films after a screening. Then she invited me to tea. Our friendship grew from there.

Fifteen years later, when I suggested that I write the story of her life, Seema hesitated. She said she wasn't important enough to have a book written about her. Then, deciding that she had witnessed many events that were part of history, she hoped her story would be her final contribution to her community.

But Seema had not finished contributing.

Living on the margins of great art and large social movements, she saw herself for most of her life as a woman who supported others, mostly men, to bring out their creative abilities. In her later years she encouraged younger women, including me, to develop our own creativity. In her advanced old age Seema finally stood for herself.

A month before she turned ninety-four, she told me that she wanted to do two things before she died—print her old photographic negatives and have a new love.

A year later, when I called to congratulate her on her ninety-fifth birthday, Seema said she was planning to have a one-woman show of her photographs, taken between 1931 and 1950. I realized that by showing her work to the public for the first time, she was revising her life story.

As I write this, Seema, now ninety-nine, is planning her fifth show of photographs. The last twenty years of her life have been intensely productive, filled with activity, friendship, and creativity. Imagining her epitaph, she said, "You can write under my name, 'She was too busy to die.'"

This book is based on many hours of conversation with Seema, her sister Tama, and other family members and friends. I began recording video and audio interviews with Seema in 1987, shortly after I met her, and I continued to do so from time to time over the next sixteen years. When we decided that I would write her biography, I interviewed Seema intensively over a period of two years and transcribed all the interviews. I also had access to interviews of Seema's mother by Jack and by Joy Gonzalez, Seema's niece. Most of Seema and Jack's papers and records had been lost when they moved to Santa Cruz, so we had to rely on memory and a few documents, as well as my supplementary research and Seema's collection of photographs.

There was so much that fascinated me about Seema's life: her political activism; her intense love affairs; her friendships with great photographers and artists; her family, a radical *mishpocheh*, a multiracial, multicultural tribe extending from Moscow to London to Boston, from New York to California. Each of these threads had the potential to become a whole story; my challenge was to weave them into a meaningful pattern.

Seema transformed her life several times and in her last decades she became a sort of oracle, with her open eyes and heart, the ways she was able to share silence as well as laughter, small talk and struggle, and the exemplary stubbornness that led to her having her first photographic show at the age of ninety-five.

"I have priorities in my mind," she told me, "and if somebody else takes over and picks out priorities for me, it makes me tired."

One of Seema's priorities was to control the way I wrote about her. But I could not relinquish control to her. As I worked with the kaleidoscope of anecdotes and images that comprised Seema's life, I realized that we would both have to surrender to a larger pattern, the story that insisted on telling itself.

images from the past

Fifty-seven . . . fifty-eight . . . fifty-nine. Just as Seema got to sixty in her silent counting, Jason, looking at his timer, lifted the print out of the tray of hypo. Everyone calls hypo "fixer" now, but Jason, a fourth-generation photographer, used the old familiar word.

"Okay Seema, I'm putting it into the wash. You can turn the light on now."

In the dim orange light, breathing in the familiar, vinegary smell of chemicals, the ninety-five-year-old woman stood up from her chair near the door and switched on the bright overhead light, peering at the print floating in the tray. As always, she felt a thrill at seeing an image on what had been the blank whiteness of the photographic paper. This was a special image, the cabin that housed her darkroom in Yosemite, enfolded in snow.

Seema first went to Yosemite to work for Ansel Adams in late spring of 1938. That winter, when the first snow began to fall, she was so excited that she ran outside in her house slippers. She was enchanted by the fairyland of snow, reminiscent of winter in the Ukraine when she was a child.

Now, as she worked with Jason on the print, it was hard to realize that almost sixty years had passed since she'd left Yosemite.

"Are you satisfied with this exposure?" Jason asked.

This was their fourth try at printing the negative, as they worked to bring out the texture and the shades of whiteness in the snow without making it too dark. They had given it forty seconds under the enlarger lamp, rather than the four to seven seconds of exposure they used for most of the other images.

She examined the photograph, noticing with pleasure how the snow balanced the dark wood.

"Yes," she said, "this is what I had in mind."

Her eyesight had deteriorated in the past decade, and she could not see anything directly in front of her. Yet under the bright light, look-ing sideways at each print rather than straight ahead, she felt that she could see clearly enough to decide whether Jason was getting the effects she wanted.

figure 2. Darkroom, Yosemite, photo by Seema
Weatherwax, ca. 1938. Courtesy of Seema Weatherwax.

"Seema, we've been working for over six hours. Are you tired?
Should we stop now?"

"I'd like to finish first, if that's okay with you."

She knew that afterward she would be exhausted. Back in her own
apartment she would relax in her reclining chair, listening to a mystery
story on an audio cassette, letting her mind drift. Her energy would
come back after an hour or two. But now she was eager to push on, to
complete the work, just as she had done in the old days.

She turned off the overhead light, and Jason put another sheet of paper into the easel as she settled back into her chair, concentrating on following his work with her negatives. She was trying to connect his electronic technology to her own experience of working intuitively.

After all these years she remembered each negative well enough to gauge approximately how long an exposure it would need, but she could no longer focus the enlarger—and besides, everything in the darkroom was set up for Jason, who was tall. Seema had never been tall—five feet one inch was her greatest height and now, with the settling of her bones, she was four feet nine inches. So, as she put it, Jason was acting as her eyes and hands.

His great-grandfather Edward Weston had been Seema's close friend; she had met Edward through his son Chan, Jason's grandfather, her partner for five years. Jason, who had learned from childhood to be meticulous in the darkroom, had a gentle way of honoring Seema's expertise. He had agreed immediately when she asked if he would help in preparing photographs for her show from her old negatives. He loved spending time with her, listening to her stories about her life, his family, her active involvement in politics, photography, women's rights, so much that overlapped his own interests. He looked at her work with understanding eyes and said she had a special way of seeing. On the few occasions when they differed about how to print something, her vote prevailed.

"It's your show," he said. "I want to do it your way."

Jason shared Seema's belief that darkroom work should bring out the original vision of the photographer.

"You see—" she showed him a photograph of a cliff, dark against a mackerel sky—"in the shadow of the cliff, the line of sparkling lights? That is what I was after."

She had never shown her photographs to Edward Weston, nor had she shown them to Ansel Adams.

She ran the darkroom in Yosemite for four years, also acting as Adams's photographic assistant. During those years she forged lifelong bonds of friendship with Ansel and Virginia Adams, Edward and Charis Weston, and Imogen Cunningham.

I admired their work so much, and I was doing it like an amateur. I didn't feel that I was a professional with my camera. I was a professional in the darkroom, but the camera work was just my own private delight.

A week before the opening, Jason arrived at Seema's apartment late in the afternoon and drove her a few blocks to a small park overlooking the harbor, where he took photographs of Seema for her show.

So that she would not have to walk on uneven ground, he drove right up to a park bench where Seema sat patiently while Jason set up his tripod. She could not distinguish the faint shimmer of the water below them from the surrounding darkness, but she could see the brightness of the western sky.

He took a dozen photographs of Seema sitting sideways on the end of the rough wooden bench in her warm padded jacket. In the image he chose for the show, she looked up to her left, smiling, her face and mane of white hair lit by the last rays of the setting sun, the grass and trees behind her melting into the twilight. On her lap she held her camera, the square-format Super Ikonta-B that she bought when she went to Yosemite.

You could imagine that she was about to lift her camera and take a photograph of the evening sky.

seema's SHOW

Jason's portrait of Seema was the first photograph I saw when I visited her show. I stood in front of it for a while, touched by the way he had captured her luminous smile. She looked responsive to those near her and also self-contained. The focus in the twilight was slightly soft, giving the portrait a dreamy atmosphere that reminded me of a photograph of Seema when she was fifteen. Eighty years later, her dark eyes were still dreaming. I was looking at a woman who was vital and alert at the very edge of life, gazing with a smile at the unknown (fig. 3).

I like the soft focus—at my age I can use some softening. You don't want to see every wrinkle and pore.

Across from the portrait of Seema with her drift of hair glowing white in the dusk, a photograph she had taken in Yosemite showed a drift of white clouds stroking the side of a granite cliff.

figure 3. Seema, Santa Cruz, ©Jason Weston, 2000.
Courtesy of Jason Weston.

The photos offered a sense of Seema looking at her immediate environment—the path through the woods, her darkroom, telephone wires in the snow, people she knew.

I think it's important to see beauty, not only in landscapes but also in machinery, in animals, in people, in every way. People need to look at beauty, because it does something for the spirit.

Seema's show opened on October 1, 2000, a sunny Sunday afternoon, at the Mulberry Gallery, set among towering eucalyptus trees a few miles from the ocean in the village of Aptos, south of Santa Cruz on California's central coast. People drifted in and out between the gallery and the sun-drenched courtyard, gazing at the photographs, carrying food and wine outside to tables surrounded by beds of purple dahlias.

The neighboring delicatessen provided a fine spread for the opening: salmon mousse molded on a platter, an assortment of breads, cheeses, fruit, and large plates of delicate pinwheel sandwiches. Any event organized by Seema would have good food, you could be sure of that.

Inside, simply matted in off-white and framed in black wood, most of the photographs hung side by side on the fresh white walls of the gallery's new alcoves. They were grouped by subject matter, from Seema's pictures of her year in Tahiti (1931–32)—through her low-key, intimate photographs of Yosemite Valley, to a series from a farmworkers' camp in 1941, to her final portraits of people, mostly children, taken between 1945 and 1950.

Despite Seema's protests, the gallery had grouped eight of her vintage prints two by two vertically on a narrow wall, so that the viewer had to peer up and down and it was impossible to see each picture clearly. These photographs were taken at the Shafter farm labor camp in Bakersfield, California, which Seema and Jack visited in 1941 with their friend Woody Guthrie, a Dust Bowl refugee himself who felt akin to the people in the camp. The photographs showed young Woody playing his guitar and singing; children of various heights posing side by side for Seema's camera; a young, freckle-faced girl; a gaunt woman proudly holding up her painting of her old home in the Midwest.

There was a scattering of photographs of various subjects taken after 1941, the year Seema left Yosemite. A line of people carried pickets during the Hollywood Strike of 1945. A two-year-old girl, bare-bottomed Lakshmi Singh, peered into a large, overturned garbage can; four-year-old Arnie Porter investigated a telephone while his grandfather, San Francisco artist Bruce Porter, watched. These marked the end of Seema's work as a photographer of people. She had stopped photographing natural scenes when she left Yosemite; by 1950 she put her camera aside, bringing it out only occasionally. She concentrated on her work in commercial film labs, supporting her husband's largely unpaid work as a writer and sharing with him a life filled with activism.

Friends and descendants of friends from Seema's Yosemite days came to her opening: Anne Adams, a little girl when Seema came to work for her parents in Yosemite Valley; Charis Wilson, a girl of nineteen newly in love with Edward Weston when Seema first met her; Imogen Cunningham's son Ron Partridge and his daughter Betsy; Jason Weston's mother, Dorothy, and his father, Ted.

Among the photographs Jason developed for the show was one taken in 1935 of his grandfather Chan as a smiling, sleepy-eyed young man, holding Seema's five-year-old niece Joy on his shoulders. Another photograph, from 1938, showed Jason's father, Ted, age eight, at the Yosemite skating rink, his arm around Joy's waist, as the two children posed for the camera, their reflections clear and sharp-edged in the smooth ice.

Halfway through the afternoon, the crowd gathered around Seema, who was clearly visible with her wild white hair. She had given some thought to what she would wear, considering whether or not to "make a photographic statement in black-and-white," she had in the end decided on comfort—a padded Chinese silk jacket over her blouse and slacks, with soft, crepe-soled shoes. At her neck she had pinned a lovely old brooch, gold filigree set with small amethysts that had belonged to her mother.

She was accustomed to introduce other people at gatherings she organized; now she was speaking for the first time in public about her own work. Her face glowed, and as she spoke people leaned forward to listen. They were young, middle-aged, old, and very old, dark-skinned, medium-brown, golden, ruddy, and pale, some elegant, some casual. A woman sat in a wheelchair; a man leaned on a walker; a few children ran about the gallery while babies were held in their parents' arms.

Seema said little about her photographs, assuming that they spoke for themselves. Instead, she told the attentive crowd how she had first learned the mysteries of the darkroom.

When her Russian Jewish family left England and moved to Boston in 1923, there was no money for her to continue her college studies in chemistry. She saw an ad for a job in a photo lab; thinking that this would have some connection with chemistry, she set out to find an address near Scollay Square in downtown Boston. She spoke briefly of this experience, but I remembered the story she'd told me.

Seema was nearly eighteen, but she looked much younger, small and slender in her best silk dress, stockings, and high-heeled shoes, wearing a wide-brimmed hat her sister Tama had made. She took the freight elevator to the fourth floor of the warehouse and opened the door to the photo lab. A round, kind-faced man came out from his cubbyhole and asked what she wanted.

When she said she was applying for the job that was advertised in the newspaper, he said, "Why don't you go and ask your mother if it's all right?"

She took the elevator back down to the street, walked around for half an hour and returned.

"My mother said it's all right."

She was hired, starting at twelve dollars a week.

Her job was to dry wet prints by placing them on a piece of canvas attached to a revolving drum. The job required speed and dexterity, and she soon mastered it; then she wanted to learn how the prints were made.

I saw this wonderful process of creation: here were pieces of paper with nothing on them, and suddenly they started to show photographs of all kinds of things. It was fascinating to see how they came up.

Photography was considered a very special profession, and here I was, an amateur, a girl, trying to sneak in. I learned a basic principle of printing, that you had to expose the sensitive paper and the negative to each other and to the light. This was what I did for the next fifty years.

In Los Angeles in the early 1930s she met Edward Weston, whose work showed her that photography could be a fine art, using meticulous developing and printing to express the artist's original vision. When Weston heard that his friend Ansel Adams needed a photographic assistant in Yosemite, he recommended Seema for the job.

As she spoke at her show about her half-century of work as a photographic technician and how she had managed to become skilled in areas that women were not traditionally allowed to enter, she charmed her audience, just as she had charmed her employers and fellow workers. Although she couldn't see anyone's face distinctly, she had a way of turning toward one person and then another that made each one feel addressed and welcomed. She concluded her talk by urging everyone to enjoy the food and to meet each other. After bringing people together in celebration and struggle for most of her life, she wasn't about to stop now.

The show was a resounding success—Seema's work enchanted visitors just as she did. In her rapport with the people and objects she photographed, and in her meticulous presentation, I saw the tantalizing seeds of what might have become a great body of work.

I asked her if she could, would she have chosen Imogen Cunningham's or Dorothea Lange's life instead of her own? She did not hesitate.

No, I would choose my life. I loved Imogen—she was a fighting woman—she had to fight every inch of the way to make a living. She didn't have any personal happiness that amounted to anything, and I do think that's very important. I never envied Imogen even though I admired her.

Dorothea Lange, I couldn't live her life, because I couldn't go out fighting with my camera. That wasn't my way of doing things.

So I don't envy them. They fought for fame and they got it. I'm glad they did because they both deserved it. But I wouldn't exchange with them, no, neither one of them.

What was it that filled Seema's life so that she was able to lay down her camera without regret? What made relationships so vitally important to her? And how was she able to come back to her old negatives so many years later and develop them with a clear memory of what she had intended when she first took them, then exhibit her work without deprecating or exaggerating its importance?

It all hinged on her ability to make the most of the present moment.

I knew Seema as a remarkable elder woman living a fully engaged life. From the photographs and art on her walls, from her stories and from her friends and family, from images of her from childhood with her same wide eyes and determined set of the mouth, I began to understand the wholeness of her life, her passion for art, nature, and ways of helping people of different backgrounds to express the deepest parts of themselves.

figure 4. "Springtime," Yosemite, photo by Seema
Weatherwax, ca. 1939. Courtesy of Seema Weatherwax.

One source of Seema's wholeness was her willingness to stop and do nothing, reconnecting herself with her body and nature. There were signs of this in early photos and the way she described herself as a "dreamer" in her childhood and youth. In her old age she took more time each day for this all-important drop into nothingness. I learned to listen to the pauses in her speech, the silences after I asked a question that eventually became more important than the words she spoke.

figure 5. Reva and Avram Aissen, Chernigov,
ca. 1902. Courtesy of Seema Weatherwax.

1

1905–29:
from chernigov to california

In one of Seema's Yosemite pictures, a single tree stands in a snowy meadow. It is early spring, with weeds poking up through the snow, and the tree bears clusters of light blossoms on its otherwise bare branches. Evergreens fringe the meadow, and beyond them the granite cliffs of Yosemite rise, half hidden by puffs of cloud (fig. 4).

Whenever I look at that picture, although I know it is black-and-white, I see pale pink. In my mind's eye, that tree is covered with the most delicate pink blossoms.

One of Seema's early memories was of a pink dress she wore when she was five years old, in Chernigov, in Ukraine, then ruled by the Russian Czar.

A child's fairytale of life in Czarist Russia unfolded from Seema's memories. The Aissen family lived in a rambling one-story house with an orchard where all kinds of fruit ripened on the trees: pears, apples, cherries, apricots; where bushes grew heavy with currants, goose-berries, and strawberries. Each summer Seema's mother skimmed the foam from jam boiling in a great copper kettle set on a tripod over a fire outside. She spread the foam on rye bread, fresh-baked in the great wood-fired kitchen oven, as the children waited with greedy, out-stretched hands.

In the winter, banks of snow higher than one's head lined the path from the house to the outhouse. Seema was wrapped in blankets one night to ride in a troika through the forest, where wolves howled and the driver said kindly, "Don't be afraid—they are far away." She was afraid, but so long as her mother and father were there with her, she felt safe.

Listening to her stories, I was struck by the contrast with my family's memories of Eastern Europe. They referred to their homeland as "the Old Country," in the way you might speak of an old, worn-out piece of clothing or furniture. Seema's childhood sounded like paradise; her parents were a blessed, unusually prosperous couple who set a standard no one could match. But outside the warmth of their family circle, the political atmosphere of Russia was stormy with revolution and counter-revolutionary terror.

CHERNIGOV

Seema's mother, Reva Abelov, grew up in a Jewish ghetto in the Ukrainian town of Nezhin, where she witnessed pogroms, systematic, terrifying attacks carried out by mounted Cossacks who smashed furniture with their wooden clubs, ripped feather pillows, beat, raped, and killed Jews. High-spirited and confident, Reva helped her older cousins to smuggle revolutionary pamphlets to factory workers before she was ten. She was fifteen, visiting relatives in Chernigov, and her cousin Avram Aissen was twenty-two when they met. Two years later Reva and Avram married, for love, as Reva's parents had done. Their first child, Freda, was born nine months and two weeks after the wedding. She was the first of three daughters; Seema came next, then Tama.

Besides our big orchard we had a vegetable garden. Father gave us radish seeds to plant, because they grew so quickly. We would watch for the little radishes to come up, then we would eat them right there in the garden, all crunchy sweet and peppery. We'd go back to Mother with dirt on our hands and faces and she'd scrub us with cool water from a bucket.

In summer when it rained, Father would let us take our shoes and stockings off and we would walk in the ruts between the vegetable rows. The water would stir up mud, and we would get our toes squishy in the nice warm mud.

figure 6. Aissen sisters, l. to r., Freda, Seema, Tama;
Chernigov, 1909. Courtesy of Seema Weatherwax.

Chernigov was a university and government center in Ukraine, the heart of the Russian Empire's western region, called the Jewish Pale, that also included Lithuania, Galicia, and Belarus. Jews were forbidden by law to emigrate east of the Pale into what was then called Great Russia, so their numbers swelled in the West. Set apart by law, limited in opportunities for education and advancement, many Jews joined conspiracies against the Czarist regime. Seema's parents were at the center of a group of radical intellectuals, students, and workers in Chernigov, and they were known for their warmth, hospitality, and courage.

Whenever Reva and Avram entertained, the little girls were allowed to stay up for as long as they could keep their eyes open, listening to grownup conversations about politics and art, and, when asked, reciting poems that they had learned by heart, with help from their father. One poem Seema remembered learning was by Nekrasov, a nineteenth-century writer and editor much admired by Lenin.

In my mind's eye, I see a lot of people milling around and a lot of talk and laughter, and I see myself reciting this poem. I would stand there and

*sort of move my shoulders from side to side, because I was bashful, but yet
I knew that I should recite.*

She liked the dramatic images in the poem, about people traveling
in winter with the wind howling and the snow in one great drift.
Morozno, frost . . .

> *Frost. The snow-covered plain shines white,*
> *The forest ahead shines black.*
> —Nikolai Nekrasov, "Red-nosed Frost"
> ("Moroz Krasnyy Nos"), 1862–63

One winter evening Seema stood near the great woodstove, its blue
and white ceramic tiles warming the large living room and the family
and friends who sat around talking, waiting to hear classical music on
the windup gramophone. Her father asked Seema to bring him the
wooden box of needles from the table near her—in her hurry she
tripped and spilled needles all over the floor then burst into tears.

"You've nothing to cry about," Avram said, but she continued to sob.

"If you don't stop, I'll have to give you a reason to cry."

Still she sobbed, and he gave her a few spanks on her bottom.

*Which was very humiliating. That was the only time he ever spanked
me. He wanted me to know that some things are not important.*

At holiday time, Seema, Freda, and Tama, dressed all in pink, with pink
stockings and pink shoes, passed plates of cake to the guests, breaking
into grins when the grownups put coins in the little bags they wore
around their necks, the bags Reva had sewed from the same pink material as their dresses, to hold Chanukah *gelt.*

*This is a holiday of light, of life. The gelt, the coins, are a gift of love
from adults to children. When I was a child, it really meant something
for people to give us kopeks—even the very poorest gave a coin, to show
their love.*

With her kopeks, Seema felt rich. She used them to buy roasted
sunflower seeds when she and her sisters walked into town to visit their
father's bookshop, accompanied by Hannah, a distant cousin who was

paid to look after them while their mother helped out in the shop. The vendor wrapped the seeds in a cone of newspaper, and the girls cracked the seeds with their teeth, spitting out the shells.

The bookshop was right in the middle of an arcade of one-story buildings with false fronts, the only paved street in Chernigov. Seema's father had created a winter scene for the window of the shop, with a peasant's hut and little animals and trees he had carved from wood. People came from miles away just to admire his display, Seema's mother said, proud of her talented husband.

One did not speak openly about the forbidden books that were kept in the back of the bookshop.

On their way home from town one day, the girls saw people putting up a barricade. Hannah and Freda grabbed Seema and Tama by their hands and hurried them along, as "there might be trouble," Hannah said. What sort of trouble? Seema wondered. But they reached home safely.

Seema retained only vague memories of the anti-Semitism that pervaded the country.

The priest's children next door called us Zhid, a derogatory word for Jew. We weren't allowed to play in each other's yard, but we would stand near the fence and play. They only called us Zhid once in a while. Then they would forget and we would play together again.

Seema and her sisters were very impressed with a house their father made out of cardboard that fitted over his head and shoulders, with whips and a noose and guns hanging from all the windows; he wore it to a protest meeting. When the police arrived to break up the meeting, the students helped him to escape, hustling him out through a back window. Later, the police arrested him. But, as he told the girls, he was respected in the town, so they gave him a lecture and let him go.

Reva's parents emigrated to England to protect her younger brothers from conscription into the Russian army. When Seema was seven, her parents decided to join them. Avram owed a fine to the government because one of his brothers had avoided the draft; he and Reva decided they would leave secretly rather than pay the fine. They sold the bookstore, sold Avram's collection of antiques, and told the girls they were going on a trip to visit their grandparents.

As their train passed through the great wheat fields of Ukraine, Seema looked eagerly to see black cartwheels of bread in the fields, as she had been told that bread came from wheat.

When the train pulled into a village station near the Polish border, the family disembarked, gathered up their bags, and walked off into the forest. It was cold and they were dressed in their warmest clothes. Avram warned the girls to be quiet as they went.

It was quite dark when they arrived at a small hut with a thatched roof. A *muzhik*, peasant, came to the door to let them in. He was small and thin and he wore a loose blouse over his pants, high boots, a little round hat on his head. His wife wore a shawl wrapped around her stooped shoulders. Inside the hut the only light came from a candle burning in front of an icon.

Tama opened her mouth to cry, but the man stopped her, saying sternly that they must be quiet, and that they would be leaving soon.

As they were about to leave, a young woman came in carrying a baby. She begged the peasant to help her get across the border, but as she had no money, he refused. Avram said he would pay for her.

The peasant carried the baby as they walked over uneven ground through thick underbrush. The young mother followed him, and the family walked behind, picking their way over roots and through brambles in the dark. Avram and Reva took turns carrying Tama, and Seema held her big sister Freda's hand. They walked, it seemed, for a very long time.

As they approached the Polish border, the baby started to whimper. The peasant put the baby to his breast to keep it quiet and the baby's mother screamed, thinking that her child was being smothered. Shots rang out in the forest.

Avram yelled, "We surrender," and they were surrounded by soldiers. The peasant ran away into the woods with the baby in his arms, and later they heard that the baby was found on the church steps and returned to its mother in prison. After that they never learned what became of them.

When the soldiers ordered them into a wagon Seema said to herself, "It will be all right—Mama and Papa will take care of it." But when they arrived at the prison, the soldiers led Avram away and Seema began to feel really scared.

The girls huddled close to Reva as a big heavy woman ordered them to take off all their clothing. She made them lift their arms, she looked through their hair, and touched them all over, touched their genitals in a way that made Seema feel sick.

They were given their clothes back and led into a brightly lit room where there were about forty women. The room stank of urine and old sweat, and the women were drunk, sick, screaming, and sobbing.

We all clung to Mother, Tama particularly, because she was the baby, and Freda and I, we stayed close to Mother because the rest of it was so alien and so scary, but we didn't feel it as if it was real. It was something out of a story.

That night they slept on boards placed across trestles. There were no blankets, and they hugged each other for warmth. Tama slept with Reva, and Seema and Freda huddled together. In the morning they took the boards and trestles down and piled them in a corner, except for one that was used as a table. They were each given a wooden spoon, and a big bowl of foul-smelling liquid was set on the table, also a loaf of bread covered with caraway seeds, which Seema thought were mouse droppings. For years, well into adulthood, Seema was nauseated by caraway seeds.

It was Passover, and some Jewish people in that town, hearing that there was a Jewish family in the prison, sent in a pot of chicken soup, which Reva and the girls shared with the other women.

A metal can standing open in one corner of the room served as a urinal. The smell was sharp and heavy, mingled with the acrid smell of the women's unwashed bodies. Once a day, male guards took them outside to a row of holes dug in the ground, and waited as they used the latrines, standing and watching all the while.

When I think of it now, Mother was lucky that she was not raped, because she was such a pretty young woman.

All the while we were in prison Mother kept reassuring us, and she kept us from seeing some of the things that we were looking at. One of the women was separated from her child and she had milk in her breasts. She was drinking her own milk. How could that happen? We knew that women breastfed their children, but we'd never known women that squirted milk into their own mouths from their own breasts. And that we saw.

They were moved twice, staying in three similar prisons for a period of about three weeks before they were reunited with Avram and the family was sent back to Chernigov in a locked train compartment, guarded by men with guns. Their house was almost empty of furniture and felt cold and strange. They camped in the house until Avram paid his fine and they were given papers to leave the country legally. They would never see Chernigov again.

For the rest of her life Seema would find it easier to identify with other people's oppression and suffering than with her own, but her memories of prison never lost their vivid, nightmarish quality. Each time she told me about their capture and imprisonment her voice dropped into a low monotone. She was exhausted afterward and needed time to replenish herself. She and Tama had compared accounts of their experience, neither one quite believing what had happened.

I checked it with Tama recently, to find out whether it was something that I thought up or dreamed, but she also remembered it.

Five years after they left for England, the Czar's regime was overthrown, news the Aissen family heard with joy. Seema was brought up in a family that opposed the oppression of peasants and Jews; she personally witnessed the brutality of the Czar's prisons; and nothing she heard or read in later years, nothing anyone said could convince her that the revolution could lead to anything so horrible as the old regime, which treated women and small girls as she and her sisters and their mother had been treated.

Leeds

They traveled from Russia across Europe by train, then by boat to England, and again by train to Leeds in Yorkshire, where Reva's parents kept a small grocery store on Roundhay Road. In her grandparents' high narrow house behind the store Seema climbed a flight of stairs for the first time in her life, her experience of buildings until then having been

figure 7. Aissen sisters, l. to r., Freda, Seema, Tama;
Leeds, 1913. Courtesy of Seema Weatherwax.

limited to the Aissens' rambling one-story house, the smaller one-story houses of relatives and friends in Chernigov, and her father's bookstore.

Soon after they arrived in Leeds, the three girls went with their aunt Esther, Reva's youngest sister, to enroll in school.

Dressed in long, fur-lined Russian coats, wearing babushkas and traditional pointed white Russian caps on their heads, the Aissen girls looked at the English schoolchildren and their teacher and the English looked back at them with suspicion. The teacher did not know what to make of their strange names. Freda, yes, the teacher had known girls named Freda, but Seema and Tamara? She looked at the girls and said, pointing to Seema, "Sophie," and, to Tama, "Tillie." She wrote the names down in her book.

No matter that there were six Tamaras and three Seemas in the family. You got used to change. Mother's parents, Bubbe and Zayde to their grandchildren, were no longer Malke and Joseph Abelov. The immigration officer had decided their names were Millie and Joseph Adelman. They didn't speak enough English to argue with him.

Seema accepted her new name, set her mouth, and determined to fit in at school. At her aunt Dveira's school in Chernigov she had learned how to learn—you just concentrated on remembering what you were told. You didn't dwell on anything in the past—your old home, your old language, your old name. You concentrated very hard on listening and doing your homework.

I was living in my own little world. One time the whole family went to a party and I didn't want to go, because I was reading a book. But the best time to do homework was when a lot was going on around me.

By the end of her first year in England Sophie Aissen was winning prizes for her schoolwork, but she never felt wholly accepted by her classmates. Freda, like Seema, studied hard and did well at school. Tama hated school and she cried about having to go. She hated being called Jew or Sheeny by her classmates, hated having to sit next to a boy, hated having to learn the English alphabet.

Meanwhile Reva and Avram, both excellent cooks, known among friends and family for their hospitality, rented a large Victorian house at 17 Brunswick Place, on a street of similarly large houses with a gate at either end, and there they opened the Continental Hotel and Restaurant. There were several other Jewish families with children living on the same street, so the Aissen girls made friends close to home.

Avram, an inveterate collector, went hunting for antiques to furnish the house. The girls were delighted when he brought home a fish tank set in the middle of an elaborate wrought-iron birdcage. He found a glass case for his butterfly collection, another to display semiprecious stones, and two pianos: one, ornately carved, was kept in the drawing room, the other downstairs, where the girls took lessons. The house had a huge living room and dining room, which became the restaurant. They rented out most of the upstairs bedrooms and gave the girls enough space in the first of the two attics for their bedroom and a playroom. The kitchen was downstairs, with several other rooms that were used by the family.

The girls ate their midday meal in the big bright dining room with the guests, and they took their other meals in privacy with the family downstairs—Reva managed to create a sense of quiet and orderliness in the family rooms no matter how many people were staying in the hotel.

Word spread rapidly about the Continental among theater people, writers, artists, and revolutionaries from all over Europe, England, and Ireland. Radical conversation filled the air, as Irishmen from Sinn Fein mingled with Yiddish actors and musicians. Bella Bellarina, a tall, elegant woman who was lead actress of the famous Yiddish theater group from Vilna, became one of Reva's good friends. When the Vilna troupe came to stay at the Continental and needed extras for their plays, the Aissen girls were recruited. They played terrified peasants in *The Dybbuk*, enjoying themselves enormously.

One of the Sinn Fein men was in hiding from the British, and the girls knew that his presence among them was an important secret. They were used to keeping secrets.

The family spent their leisure time walking in the countryside, along fields bordered by low stone walls, past sparkling streams where brown trout swam. In spring and summer they gathered bouquets of wild flowers.

Despite, or perhaps because of his revolutionary beliefs, Avram was fascinated by English castles; he carved elaborate miniature castles of wood, which the girls were allowed to play with before the castles were sold to admiring customers.

When war began in 1914, school was cut to half-sessions, to make room in the school buildings for soldiers. Concerned for the girls' education, Avram enrolled them in the Nationale Radicale Schule, which they attended every Sunday, learning Yiddish, reading the stories of Sholem Aleichem and Sholem Asch, imbibing a culture that would stay with them all their lives.

Religion was another matter.

Seema was offended when she and her sisters were kept out of the Sukkoth, the charming little house of boughs her grandparents built in their backyard each autumn for the harvest festival of Sukkot. The girls were allowed to eat their meals inside the Sukkoth only when there was room—adults and their boy cousins were given preference. Their grandparents doted on all the children, but when it came to matters of religious observance, the boys, even the babies, had clear priority.

She argued with her aunt Esther about this and other matters. In the synagogue, the women and girls sat upstairs in a small balcony, watching, while the men and boys prayed, chanted, and danced downstairs. Both grandparents worked hard all week in the grocery store, but Bubbe, the grandmother, also cooked and cleaned, working hard to have everything ready for the Sabbath before sundown on Friday night. Then, until sundown on Saturday, you couldn't even tear a piece of paper or light a lamp or a stove. Bubbe tied a handkerchief to her sleeve each Sabbath, because she was not allowed to carry anything.

Esther listened when Seema objected to these customs, replying simply that it was a matter of faith. But Seema saw that her parents, who were not religious, had a more equal relationship than her grandparents.

After three successful years, Reva and Avram decided to close their hotel. The work was unremitting, and besides, Reva said, she hated having to charge for hospitality. Friends helped Avram get started in the textile industry, buying cloth from manufacturers and selling it to retailers, and he soon had a thriving business. Both Reva and Avram were active in organizing support for the new Soviet Union, and they often took the girls to benefit concerts and lectures for the Bolshevik cause. These were exciting times, when artists, writers, and musicians were inspired with revolutionary fervor. Despite their hard-won middle-class status, the Aissen family always identified themselves with the working class, and they taught their girls to do the same.

As his business prospered, Avram enrolled all three of the girls in the Girls' Modern School, a middle-class Leeds establishment, where Seema was generally acknowledged to be extremely bright, especially in math and science. She played on the school basketball team, but most of all she loved gymnastics, climbing ropes, learning back flips, and other graceful strenuous exercises that she would continue to practice through her adult years.

In the summers Reva took the girls to Ilkley, a resort town outside Leeds, where they rented rooms from two spinsters who became family friends. Reva taught the Englishwomen to make borscht, and Tama won their hearts with her enthusiasm for boiled new-laid eggs. Avram joined them on weekends, and as they strolled to the waterfall at Haber's Gill, admiring the flowers on the stream bank, the water rushing over bright stones, and their daughters walking ahead in light summer dresses, Reva and Avram told each other that they had been right to leave Russia, considering all the chaos there, with the Allies fighting to overthrow the Bolsheviks and civil war ravaging the Ukraine. Most of Avram's family had also left Russia, emigrating to Boston and writing letters about the good life in America.

During the war there was rationing in England and troops were everywhere; bombs fell on nearby villages; the family burned furniture and old clothes from the attic to keep warm. Reva's brother Barney hid in the attic to avoid the draft, because Lenin had issued a warning that Russians abroad should not fight on the side of the "imperialists." Seema and her sisters carried food up to their Uncle Barney and they also took part in the war effort, knitting scarves for British soldiers.

In 1918, as the war was ending, a pandemic of influenza swept over England, Europe, and the United States, killing millions of people. All the Aissens fell ill and took to their beds. Thirteen-year-old Seema stayed by her father, who was feverish, hallucinating. When their neighbor Doctor Umansky came to visit late that night, he didn't stay long; he shocked Seema by brusquely declaring as he left that Avram would die soon. Seema sat by her father's door for most of the night, trembling, as the nurse came and went and then her mother appeared like a ghost, crying for her dead husband. Avram Aissen died on November 9, two days before the Armistice was declared.

The next day, as family and friends filled the house with the sounds of their grief, Seema did not cry. But at night, in her bed, small moans came out of her, and she heard them as if they came from someone else. She felt abandoned, alone as never before. Once, when she met Tama in the hall, the two sisters held each other close and cried. Otherwise, each of the sisters kept her grief to herself.

One of their father's friends told fifteen-year-old Freda: "You are the man of the family now." Freda immediately left school to help Reva support the family; she would dedicate her life to her mother and sisters.

Reva slid into a heavy depression. Finally, realizing that there was no one else to look after the girls, she roused herself to take over Avram's textile business. She succeeded by sheer force of will despite the prejudice against her, an attractive young widow in a male-dominated industry, and she was soon able to buy a comfortable house for herself and her daughters. She spoke of wallpapering the parlor in black to show that she was still in mourning, but the girls talked her out of it. Freda helped Reva with the business and mothered the two younger girls. It was Freda with whom Seema discussed her problems with teachers, Freda who helped Seema with the mysteries of her first menstruation, and, later on, her first encounters with boys.

Seema was the first to cut her hair short, shocking her mother, but soon her sisters followed her example. Freda's hair waved demurely and Tama's sat close to her head, but Seema had a wild curly bush.

I was supposed to be such a good little girl, so Mother was amazed that I did such a powerful thing.

By fifteen she had blossomed into extravagant beauty, her wild hair accentuating the soft curves of her face and her dark eyes. Without telling her, Reva sent off a photograph of her middle child in her favorite gray silk dress with short sleeves, her curly hair subdued by a headband, her cheek resting on her hand, to a beauty competition. Seema was selected as a finalist, and then a letter arrived, saying that she was not eligible to win the contest, because she was not "of English background."

When she graduated from high school and won a scholarship to college, Seema convinced the local school board to let her go to the technical college. She was fascinated by math, physics, and chemistry, and chose the last as the most practical way to earn her living, as she could not imagine undertaking the long course of study leading to a career in research. The men on the board, all sitting in a solemn row behind a long table, suggested she go to business school or learn home economics, but pretty young Seema answered all their questions patiently and sweetly, insisting that chemistry was what interested her. She became the only woman studying science full-time, and she did well in the college.

Now that she was a grownup college student, Seema began to date. A boy they called Wuffles, who came from a well-to-do family, impressed her with his charming manners and his dancing. He was the only boy she knew who had his own car. He took her to tearooms to dance, and he came to her house when the sisters had tea parties, all gathering around the piano to sing. Seema wondered if he would ask her for a kiss. If he were to ask, she thought, she might agree, just to find out what kissing was all about. But then, a kiss was such a commitment, so she was relieved that he never asked. He was, after all, a perfect gentleman.

Seema knew there was no future for her with Wuffles. He never introduced her to his family, and he was a snob. One day, as they passed a beggar on the street, Wuffles made a sneering remark that grated on Seema. She never told him, as they walked past the grocery on the corner of Roundhay Road, that it belonged to her grandparents, but she disliked herself for the omission.

Wuffles was not the only young man in her life. There was a tall, quiet boy who loved poetry and hiking and carried a camera with him wherever he went. He took photographs of her among fields of daffodils, in front of lilac bushes in bloom, under mimosa trees heavy with fuzzy yellow buttons; when she left England he sent her a book he had made with the photographs accompanied by poems of Wordsworth, Shelley, and Keats. She treasured the book and grieved when it was lost, but in her nineties, thinking back through the years, she could not remember his name, only Wuffles.

Freda was immensely popular with a string of suitors who turned to Seema for consolation when Freda rejected them. Tender-hearted Seema fell in love with each of them, only to transfer her affections to the next desolate young man. Her favorite was a tall, red-haired medical student called Ginger, who came one day in search of Freda and found Seema lying on the couch with a violent headache.

Ginger held her hand and stroked her head, and the headache went away.

I thought to myself, "This boy has healing powers—he must become a doctor."

tHE DREamER

Seema's life at this point seemed like a radical Jewish version of *Little Women*. She and her sisters and mother were close-knit and idealistic, struggling to make their way in life as a family. The loss of Avram had caused a dramatic shift; they abandoned their Friday night tradition of family dinners with white tablecloth and napkins, thick soup and a pot roast with potatoes and vegetables, fresh *challah* (braided egg bread), one of Reva's fine strudels or a sponge cake for dessert, and the Sabbath candles ready to light on the sideboard in case Reva's mother should drop by unannounced. Those dinners had been bright, with everyone talking and joking, but after Avram's death Friday night was like any other night, except for the tinge of grief.

Nonetheless, the sisters made their own traditions in the lovely house that Reva bought: in summer they waded into fields of bluebells, gathering armfuls of flowers for the table; there were tea parties at which the girls entertained their friends, all gathering around the piano

figure 8. Aissen sisters, l. to r., Tama, Seema, Freda; Leeds, 1920. Courtesy of Seema Weatherwax.

to sing together, where Seema learned to smoke and dropped ashes that burnt a hole in the front of her yellow velvet dress; there were adventures, like the time when Freda and Seema went off to walk all day in the Yorkshire countryside and prove to their friends that they could fast for Yom Kippur, only to break their fast at sundown with a hearty, decidedly unkosher country tea of ham and eggs; or the time when Seema had a serious infection in her arm and Freda's patient nursing saved her from having to have the arm amputated.

The family was a crucial container for Seema, and yet her dreaming path led elsewhere. Once, looking for the pattern that wound its way like a river through her life, I asked Seema if she remembered any early dreams. She didn't remember any dreams from childhood; furthermore, she said tartly, she didn't need to have her dreams analyzed. However,

There was a dream I had over and over. It started when I was a young woman, and it went on throughout most of my life. I had it again a few years ago.

I was with a bunch of people at some event. We were family, or friends, and the place was indoors, or out, always an enclosure of some kind.

Suddenly, I looked around, and all my friends were gone. I kept looking, and I realized I had no way to get home. I felt panicky, because everyone left without me.

This dream makes me think of the time my father died—I felt abandoned by him.

In 1921 a depression hit England's textile and railroad industries. Reva's business failed. Unable to earn a living, she decided to sell her house and take her daughters to Boston, where Avram's family had promised to help set her up in a new business. Freda put aside her romance with a young medical student, Paul, hoping to return and marry him once the others were established. But things were not as rosy as they had thought, and they all struggled to earn a living in Boston. Seema and Tama both told me that Freda never really recovered from her separation from Paul. She never returned to England, and she never regained her early vitality.

Ten years later, Reva went back to England for a visit. Paul came to see her, asking about Freda, who had married Frank. He cried, confessing that he still loved Freda deeply. When Seema asked Freda why she did not go back with Reva, Freda said, "I have changed so much, and I'm afraid to see him changed also." And that was all. She never spoke of him again.

For Seema at seventeen, the departure from Leeds and the sea voyage to Boston were a great adventure. She was curious about America, curious about boys and clothes and what was to come. Reva had bought second-class tickets with money from the sale of their house in Leeds, and Seema and Tama danced their way across the Atlantic. Once, Seema accompanied a man to his stateroom, and she was about to explore the mysteries of kissing.

The door flew open, and Mother came in. She gave me hell!

Mother didn't realize I was doing an experiment. She thought I was being seduced. I wouldn't have done any more than find out what a kiss was like. So anyway, that was the end of that.

BOSTON

When they arrived in Boston Harbor, Seema saw a crowd of people waiting behind an iron fence. She had seen people chewing gum in American movies; even so, she was amazed at the sight of so many mouths moving back and forth, rhythmically, like a bunch of cows, she thought.

Riding in their Uncle Adolph's car, they left the pier district, passing warehouses and deserted streets where they saw drunks staggering in an alleyway, the alcoholic face of Prohibition.

The entire Boston Aissen clan waited to greet them at their Aunt Seema's house in Roxbury, a duplex with an upstairs flat where they would stay until they found their bearings. Twenty-two people sat around the table eating chicken soup, everyone speaking at once. The Aissens were different from the Abelovs, more politically engaged, not religious, more intellectually inclined. Reva and her children were warmly embraced by Avram's family, and Seema felt more at home here than she had with her beloved grandparents in England.

Five of Avram's ten siblings were there, with their spouses and children; for the first time the girls met cousins their own age: Louis Gilbert, who had lost his leg in a bicycle accident; and Liza (pronounced Liz-uh), just out of high school, who became Seema's best friend.

Seema hoped to continue in college, like her Boston cousins and their circle of friends who were at MIT, Harvard, and Boston College. But her credits from England were not transferable; she had no scholarship here, and there was no money for her education.

It was the first time that I realized that it took money to go to school, because I was never involved in the finances of the family. I discovered that in order to get by I would have to go to work, so I started to think about economics in relation to my own life.

My uncle thought that I, as a young woman, should do a business course, but I did not want that. So without really fighting him, I had to get out of going to business school, or taking a job in an office.

She started reading ads in the newspaper and found her first job in a photography lab, where she soon mastered her task of feeding finished prints onto a canvas drum to dry.

figure 9. L. to r., Seema, Reva, Tama Aissen, Boston, 1928.
Courtesy of Seema Weatherwax.

She worked in a big room with a wall of windows at one end that looked out over the street below. At the other end of the room was a black curtain, and it was from behind that curtain that people emerged carrying wet prints for her to dry, or strips of negatives that they hung from hooks in a large wooden booth. Once dried, the negatives were cut and sorted into wooden cubbyholes on the wall, where they were matched by number to the dry prints.

As if on purpose to rescue her from boredom, one day a man came out from behind the black curtain and motioned her to follow him. She was curious as she went through the curtain and turned right and then left, into a darkened room lit by a single yellow-green light. There she saw two women sitting at a table with large trays of clear liquid where pieces of paper floated. There was a door at the end of the room. Telling Seema to wait, the man went through that door and returned, carrying a wooden frame with glass on one side, black paper, and a 5 × 7 negative.

He placed the negative on the wooden base, then he placed a piece of photosensitive paper over it, showing her which side of the paper had emulsion.

"You must be sure that the emulsion side of the paper is touching the emulsion side of the negative," he told her.

Then he put the glass on top, and fastened the box. He covered the glass with the black paper.

"Take this out to the window and expose it to the light for thirty seconds. You will need to count, like this, one . . . two . . . Then bring it back to me."

She did exactly as she was told, then back in the darkroom she watched curiously as the man took the paper out of the box and handed it to one of the women, who put it into a big developing tray. The manager called Seema back into the main room before she could see the print emerging from the developer. From then on, whenever she could, she stole into the first of the two darkrooms to watch the women at their work.

She learned the basic principles of contact printing and developing by observation, watching carefully as a negative was placed next to sensitive paper in the printer and exposed to light for a certain amount of time, and then the paper was put into the tray of developer. She saw the women wait, counting, as the image emerged, and just at the right time they pulled out the print, which then went into the tray of fixer and another of washer.

She never got as far as the second room, where the men worked in absolute darkness to develop film, nor did she see them using the enlargers. They had nothing big enough for 5 × 7 prints, which rarely came in, hence her assignment to expose the larger photosensitive paper to daylight.

There was an air of secrecy about photofinishing that made Seema all the more determined to learn the craft.

Newcomers weren't encouraged—my job was to dry prints, not to learn what the professionals were doing.

After a year and a half in her first photo lab job, she felt ready to try something more challenging. She answered an ad for someone experienced in developing and printing, to work in a gift shop in Malden, half an hour by trolley from Boston. She spoke in confident tones to the couple who owned the gift shop, telling them that she was just the person for their new photo lab, as she had been working in a photofinishing lab for over a year now. They hired her along with a young man who was to develop film and do enlargements.

Seema and her young male colleague worked together to master the skills of photofinishing. They filled wastebaskets with their mistakes at first, but as they figured out the correct timing, the waste diminished and their successes increased.

Meanwhile, she was asking herself why the young man was hired for the essential work of film developing while she was hired for the less important work of developing paper. After all, they were equally inexperienced. Men, she concluded, were automatically hired to do the important work. At this point, she contented herself with learning how to print.

It's a seeing process. You look at a negative and you think, "This negative does not have enough contrast, and in order to bring out contrast it should go on this paper." Then you look at another negative and it is exactly even, it doesn't have to have any special help, so there's a medium paper; or, there's another paper if it's too contrasty.

At the same time that you're gauging that, you say, "Okay, the negative looks like it's very thin, so maybe it should take only three or four seconds." You can't just put it in the developer and pull it out any time you feel like it. You have to know, but until you know, you guess. You make incorrect guesses, then you try again. When something develops before your eyes because of your own efforts, it's enjoyable, a creative process.

At home, there was always a large noisy family scene. The Aissens spilled in and out of each other's houses—there was always room to sleep on a couch or on the floor, always enough food for anyone who showed up at the table.

The older members of the Aissen family had vivid memories of anti-Semitism and oppression under the Czarist regime in Russia, and they were thrilled by the apparent success of the Bolshevik Revolution. In Boston they saw workers being bullied on the picket lines by goons and police, and they dreamed of another revolution that would lead America to the socialist ideal they believed was being carried out in Russia.

Party meetings at Workman's Hall in Roxbury resembled family gatherings, as there were so many Aissens present. As always, whether crowded around a dinner table or sitting on folding chairs in a bare hall, they liked to speak all at once, each one passionately arguing for his or her viewpoint.

After a year of attending meetings and demonstrations and reading and reflecting on such classic texts as Marx's *Value, Price and Profit*, Seema joined the recently formed Young Communist League, started secretly in 1922 in Bethel, Connecticut, for young adults like herself, many of them immigrants or children of immigrants.

Some of her friends were members; others were not, either from a lack of interest in politics, or because they were fearful of being expelled from their schools or jobs or deported from the country, as thousands of immigrants were during the notorious Palmer Raids. The Immigration Act of 1920 had made the possession of Communist literature or the expression of support by non-naturalized immigrants a punishable action. Although Seema was aware of the persecution of Communists, activism was an exciting adventure for her, serving ideals she had learned from her earliest years.

The conflicts inside the Party were never more significant to her than arguments among family members—it often seemed to amount to the same thing. One wouldn't repudiate Communism any more than one repudiated one's own family, or one's Jewish background. That didn't mean you agreed with everything the Party said or did.

At that time it was considered petit bourgeois to get dressed up or to act too feminine. But we dressed like the rest of the world—we didn't put on leather jackets—we were not trying to downgrade our lives, we were trying to upgrade. There was no problem, as far as we were concerned, in dressing as nice as we could. So we were frowned upon. But we still were active—we did what we thought was right.

With their cousins, Seema and Tama drove around the city in a rented truck, painting slogans on billboards in support of the Communist presidential candidate.

Four or five of us went around at midnight with a stencil writing Vote for William Z Foster *on billboards all over the city. A couple of times the patrols chased us. We had a bucket of red paint sloshing over, and we'd get on these billboards, you know, sometimes you had to climb a little bit, and we'd hear an approaching car. We would hop in the truck and drive away. They never did catch us, so we were never put in jail.*

I want you to understand, these young people that I was with, our cousins and their friends, they were not narrow in their interests. We did everything—we went to the opera, the symphony, we went to ballets. We went to hear this guy where we had to sit on the floor and say Om. We went to see Anna Pavlova do one of her swan dances, supposedly her last performance—she did that three or four times.

We used to buy one ticket for the gallery and several of us would use it—one would hand it on to another in the crowd. The ticket was for standing up only, and you looked down at the main floor and saw which seats were empty. Then, came a break, you sat down in a nice seat. That's how we could afford it.

The night they saw Pavlova dance, Jack Weatherwax from Aberdeen, Washington, an undergraduate student at Harvard, was also present, but he and Seema would not meet for another sixteen years.

marriage

There were three interwoven threads in Seema's life in the mid-1920s: work, the YCL, and social life, influenced in style and pace by the Jazz Age. Seema liked to joke with me that she was the quintessential Party Girl; in the years I knew her she was always busy organizing parties, from large fundraisers to impromptu gatherings in her apartment. In their first year in Boston, Seema and Tama together with their cousin Liza organized a social club called the Cheerful Cherubs, which met in the attic of Aunt Seema's house. In their honor, Uncle Oscar painted a mural of floating cherubs on the attic ceiling, which impressed them all enormously.

We used to put on shows, and we put out this magazine, with articles, drawings, and jokes . . . we did all sorts of creative, crazy things until we started to fall apart by getting married, one by one.

> A C.C.C. [Cheerful Cherub's Club] Song
> Sing a song of flappers
> Big and thin and small
> Hiking all together
> Not heeding cry or call . . ."
> etc. etc. etc.
> This is the beginning of a C.C.C. song.
> We want you to supply more verses, even one will do.
> . . . .
> You will certainly find us interested and sympathetic . . .
> All attempts will be held as strictly private.
> We reserve all rights to judge the entries.
> Editors. S. Aissen
> A. Goldstein
> —from the first issue of *The Cherubite*

Seema attracted boyfriends easily, first in Leeds and again in Boston, but she remained ignorant about sex. As a precocious adolescent encouraged by her father to read widely, she had read novels by D. H. Lawrence,

figure 10. James Lacey and Seema, Boston,
ca. 1925. Courtesy of Seema Weatherwax.

Tolstoy, and Dostoevsky; sex for her was an abstract idea, a thrilling romantic adventure with no physical reality, no connection with anything she knew.

Seema and Tama were invited on a double date, canoeing on the Charles. They had rowed on the river in Leeds, and they agreed eagerly.

"Are you good sports?" the men asked.

"Of course we are." And so they went up to the canoe rental office. Soon they were off on the river. When they came to a wooded area the men helped the sisters out, each man leading his partner to a grassy sheltered spot, with some distance between the couples.

They started to grope, wanting to have sexual play, trying to feel our breasts. We understood that something more was going to happen— exactly what it would be we didn't know, but we knew it was not what we wanted. They took us back, but they were very angry and said we led them on, because we told them we were "good sports." Of course we didn't understand what they meant. That was when we found out that words in English and in American did not always mean quite the same.

During her second winter in Boston, Seema met a handsome older man, a Boston Irishman named James Lacey who was active in the movement. He was a mentor to the younger YCL members and Seema was flattered and impressed by his interest in her. They soon paired off, and the following summer they spent several weekends, along with other friends, visiting Freda, who was running a country retreat on an old farm.

The only place for us to sleep was in the barn, and so there we'd be, Ben and Lillian, Zeke and Polly—I don't think Tama was dating that way yet with the man that she married. Most of us young progressives thought it didn't matter whether you had a marriage certificate or not. We did believe that one should have a stable relationship with a person of the opposite sex.

Jim and I didn't have real sex before we were married. It was pleasurable, it was nice in every way, but it wasn't sex. When he started to caress me, I was open to, what shall I say, first sexual advances. I can't say that I was aroused, but my curiosity was aroused. I was not aware of the sexual act, what it really involved. So, we had this fondling relationship for a while, and then he wanted to get married.

Reva was convinced from the start that Jim Lacey was not a good match for Seema, but in 1925, over her mother's strong protests, Seema married Jim.

We had to overcome my mother's tears. I believed that I knew what I was doing, and the more people spoke against it the more I wanted to marry Jim.

So we went to a justice of the peace and we got married. Afterward, he tried to act like a husband and to have sexual intercourse. The whole process upset me. I was very shocked about it.

Seema had also to deal with her new duties as wife to a man who expected that she would be responsible for their meals. She had never managed a household and she knew nothing about budgeting.

I found out that you couldn't eat steak at the beginning of the week and then have anything left at the end.

By the end of the week Seema and Jim were often left with only cornflakes in their cupboard. She avoided visiting her family when she was hungry, knowing Reva would invite her to eat with them and not wanting her mother to see her eagerness at the dinner table.

PATERSON, NEW JERSEY

At a Boston gathering a man named Reilly offered Seema a job in Paterson, New Jersey, operating a Photomat machine in a department store. Just to avoid any problems, Reilly said casually, he suggested that Seema write "S. Aissen" on the job application. She had to clean and maintain the machine, making sure that the supply of chemicals was kept fresh—it was a job she could do easily and well. Thinking that a change of scene might help her marriage, Seema talked to Jim, who was interested in the union struggles going on in New Jersey among the textile workers. At that time he could easily find odd jobs, painting houses and hanging wallpaper, and so they decided to move.

The Party wanted Seema and Jim to stay in Boston, but Seema didn't believe it was necessary to ask for permission where her private life was concerned. She had a number of disagreements with Party policies,

figure 11. House in Paterson, New Jersey, photo by Seema
Weatherwax, ca. 1928. Courtesy of Seema Weatherwax.

especially the cult of personality, amounting to near-worship of Lenin
and later Stalin, but she was able to disagree and remain involved, a pattern she would follow through most of her life.

They rented a small house with a large, private backyard, and
Seema enjoyed buying new wicker furniture. There was no hot water,
only a cold shower in the basement, and in the summer, when it
rained, she went out into the backyard with a bar of soap to bathe in
the warm rain. On the face of it, things were fine. But there was no sub-
stance to the marriage.

*I had no emotional or sexual response to Jim, and he did not know how
to make me respond. Obviously we were not suited to each other. We tried
and tried to make a marriage out of it, and it just did not work.*

*Perhaps if he had understood the need to have a longer period . . . But
how could he understand that, because I wasn't talking about it? I never
tried to explain what my real feeling was. I felt that I couldn't insult him.
If this was what was supposed to happen, then there was something wrong
with me. I hadn't grown up yet.*

Jim began to stay out most evenings and then Seema was alone for the first time. Her voice took on a bleak tone as she spoke about that period.

Soon after Seema and Jim left Boston, Tama married Al Sands, a radical speaker and organizer whose parents also came from Ukraine.

"He's a *landsman*," she told Reva, who was worried about her youngest daughter, "You don't know him, but you know his parents. They were in Siberia. He's one of us." Tama and Al moved to New York, where they prevailed on Reva to join them. Reva, who had taught herself how to make slipcovers in Boston, was able to earn a living working for a New York department store, but she worried about her daughters: Seema because she was evidently unhappy in her marriage, Tama because Al put his movement work ahead of earning a living. Freda, Reva felt, would take care of herself: she had paired off with Ben Brown, a big Hungarian they all called Brownie.

Remembering those far off days, Tama, who had her own opinions about people and events in their shared past, said that Brownie was "a nutty guy—you couldn't talk seriously to him. He was attractive but there was nothing to him." She was even more succinct in her opinion of James Lacey. "He was a louse."

Freda and her partner Brownie lived for a while with Seema and Jim in Paterson, and they all took part in the strikes and demonstrations that marked those early years of labor organizing. On weekends they took the train into New York to visit Reva and Tama and attend concerts, despite Seema's claustrophobia, which led her to dread every trip through the Hudson River tunnel. She would sit very still as the train roared through the darkness, trying not to imagine what would happen if the tunnel caved in.

One morning in 1928, two men in business suits came up to Seema at the photo machine and asked where they could find S. Aissen.

"I'm S. Aissen."

"We're looking for the S. Aissen who runs this machine."

"That's me."

"But you're a woman! We can't have a woman doing this job."

I was fired on the spot. We went through a long talk about the fact that there were absolutely no errors, no beefs, but just because I was a woman, I couldn't hold a job like that. I knew beforehand that there were special jobs for men, even from my first job, but this was open discrimination. That was my first run-in in the labor field.

CROSS-COUNTRY

Word was drifting east about the beauty of southern California, where the sun shone all year. In April of 1928, Tama and Al, Seema and Jim, and Reva set out for California. Al had been asked by the Party to teach at a workers' school in Seattle: the plan was that they would drive first to Los Angeles, where they had a cousin who would help Seema, Jim, and Reva to get settled; then Al and Tama would rejoin them once Al had finished his work in Seattle. Freda and Brownie said they would come out west later.

Each of the five contributed two hundred dollars cash to the expenses of the trip, and they took camping equipment and food along with

figure 12. Seema with Jim's Ford in California, 1929. Courtesy of Seema Weatherwax.

them. The women each took one nice outfit—a dress, fancy shoes, and stockings; and a change of traveling clothes—pants and a sweater. They expected to be on the road for several weeks, as Al had some speaking engagements along the way.

Reva sewed dresses and coats for the three women, which she packed in crates along with their other belongings to send out west. Four crates were left in the basement of Tama and Al's apartment house in New York.

Al was given an old Model-T Ford, an open car, for the trip.

That beautiful car, which was one of those old Ford touring cars, you know, with floppy sides and everything, anyway, as soon as it left New York, it saw a garage. So it broke down. And from then on every time it saw a garage it broke down.

One evening, after about two weeks on the road, they were up to their ankles in thick mud, helping to push the car off the railroad tracks where it had stalled. They didn't know if or when a train might come along, and it was dark. They tried standing on top of the tracks, but their feet kept slipping.

Jim did very little to help. "It's Al's car, let him take care of it," he muttered.

Their cash fund dwindled rapidly, and Jim's moroseness grew with their troubles. They were living rough, camping by the side of the road, eating as cheaply as possible. Sometimes they were able to stay with movement people in the towns where Al spoke.

Al had engagements in different towns, and so we traveled sometimes into the night to reach a certain town. This one time we stopped at a gas station in the countryside. There was a young man there, and he said he'd just been held up an hour before, at gunpoint. Up to that time the police had not been able to find these robbers. So we, the three women in the car, said, "We oughtn't to go now, until they catch them." And the guys said, "Oh no, everything's okay." The only weapon we had was an axe, for camping. They put the axe in the front of the car.

It took us a good half hour to get out of the station, because all three women were scared stiff, and I remember us taking turns going to the bathroom, one after the other.

We started to drive, and we hadn't gone more than fifteen minutes before, Boom! a big bang, and we thought, Aha! we've been shot at. No, it was a flat tire. So, the guys got out to fix it. The tire had a nail in it, and they put a patch on it and tried to ride it, thinking it would last, but it wouldn't last. There were eight flat tires that evening, before we got to the town.

Al was an excellent speaker, able to engage crowds of working people with his thoughtful analysis of the capitalist system, as he explained why the system was unjust and how workers could unite to struggle against the system. Although the country was officially in boom time, several key industries, like textiles, had already failed, and many people were unemployed.

By the time they reached Kansas City, the others were disgusted with Jim's moodiness and lack of cooperation. Jim was jealous of Al's stature in the movement and his happy marriage to Tama—frustrated by his own inability to contribute anything tangible and by his unfulfilling relationship with Seema.

His character changed to a certain extent. When I married him he was a pretty good man, but he became bitter, because he expected a wife and he wasn't getting one.

I still had the idea, which was instilled in all women of that period, that you marry and you have two children, a boy and a girl, and you live happily ever after. And if you don't, then it's the woman's fault, because she's doing something wrong, or she's frigid.

Seema and Jim decided to stay behind in Kansas City and earn money to finish their trip to California by bus. Reva, Tama, and Al went ahead, with very little cash and a few cans of food in their recalcitrant car. Al would be able to raise a little money with his lectures. They left, thinking that Seema and Jim would stay with their cousin Reva, Aunt Henya's daughter from Boston, who was newly married. Seema assured them that soon she and Jim would earn enough money to continue west.

It would take the unhappy couple nine months to complete their journey to Los Angeles. After her family left them in Kansas City, Jim disappeared for a while. Cousin Reva and her husband lived in a one-room flat, and it was impossible for Seema to stay there after the first few nights, so she found herself temporarily homeless. She camped out at the union hall, sleeping on a pile of lice-infested clothing collected for strikers' families. When Jim reappeared several days later, having found a room where they could stay, she asked no questions.

I was so unhappy about the relationship that I didn't even try to find out what the heck he was doing. It's my belief that he was trying to satisfy his needs by being active in the labor struggle, and that he just gave up on trying to make a living.

In Kansas City Seema met Ella Reeve Bloor, "Mother Bloor," the charismatic Communist labor leader who was then in her sixties, hitchhiking across the country, distributing the *Daily Worker* and organizing farmworkers. At that time the average annual wage for industrial workers was about $1,300, and farmworkers earned even less, while the poverty level for a family of four was set at $2,000. Poor people suffered from the country's economic imbalance for years before the Depression was official, and there was widespread interest in unions.

Mother Bloor asked Seema to introduce her when she spoke on street corners, standing on the traditional soapbox. She told Seema a little about her background, that she came from a prominent middle-class family, that she had decided to join the Communist Party and enter public life as a labor organizer.

She was very straightforward, and she spoke directly to people about what was going on. She had a number of health problems by then from the hard life she'd led, and it was courageous of her to speak on a soapbox. She spoke openly as a Communist, and that was really something.

After she spoke, Mother Bloor invited people to go to Party headquarters. Seema accompanied her, and several young men came along, which delighted the organizers.

But the young men were not interested in joining the Party, and they had not come because of Mother Bloor.

The young men were all propositioning me, because they had heard that there was free love in the Movement. They came because I was cute and I was different, so after the second or the third time I said to the organizers, "I am not going to introduce anybody."

Seema and Jim scraped along, more apart than together. In Kansas City, after months of looking for work, she got a job as cashier in a five-and-dime store; in Omaha she worked as a waitress until an ex-convict with a gun tried to persuade her to go away with him, whereupon she quit her job and stayed home for several weeks, afraid he would track her down. In Phoenix she was ill with the flu and sat on the front step of their little shack in the desert sun, wrapped in a blanket, hoping that the sun would heal her. When she recovered she answered an ad by a portrait photographer who wanted help in her darkroom; she wore the one good dress she had brought with her from Paterson.

It was a nice cotton, with a little flower design, pretty form-fitting. It was the only dress I had, and I used to wash it after a few days' wear. Over the months it got a little bit shorter. Because I was wearing this short dress and high heels, and had an accent, everybody including this woman right away said, "Are you French?" I just smiled prettily and nodded my head and let it go.

The portrait photographer paid her no wages, but Seema worked for the experience; she earned some cash relieving an elevator operator in the same building. Jim got a few odd jobs; somehow they found places to stay and a little money for groceries, and Seema didn't inquire what Jim was doing. The Depression was around the corner for the country, but it was full-blown in their relationship.

We starved a little bit in Kansas City, then we went and starved in Omaha, Nebraska, for three months, and then we went to Phoenix, Arizona, where we finished this whole process. This was in '28, right at the beginning of the Depression. It already had hit, but people were not jumping out of windows, like they did in '29. But at that time there were no jobs.

After three months in Phoenix Seema and Jim met a man who was driving a big truck to California, and he agreed to give them a ride. He was recently widowed with three children, and he had sold his farm in the Midwest after his wife died.

He answered an ad that said, BEAUTIFUL CITRUS PROPERTIES AVAILABLE. Hundreds and hundreds of people sent money for this beautiful property where they were going to pick grapefruit and oranges and lemons and make a fortune. When he got to Arizona, the plants were just a few inches high. It would take years for them to even have one piece of fruit, and he had put all his money into that.

He had a big open truck, and the little girl sat in the front with him. We were in the back with the two older kids, and he spread blankets for us to sleep on. After we got to Los Angeles and unloaded, he told us that his original idea was to drive over the side of a cliff, because he felt there was no future for him or the kids. Had we not been in the truck with him, he said, he would have gone over, but he felt responsible for us.

He never kept in touch with us and there was no way we could keep in touch with him, because he had no sense of where he was going. It's very sad, how many things like that must have happened during that period.

figure 13. Seema, Los Angeles,
ca. 1930. Courtesy of Seema Weatherwax.

2

1929–38:
Los angeles, tahiti, Los angeles

Los angeles

THE CLEAR BLUE SKIES AND ORANGE GROVES OF LOS ANGELES LOOKED like heaven to Seema. Reva had found a job making slipcovers and had begun to settle into the community of Boyle Heights, known as the Bronx of Los Angeles to Jewish radicals arriving from the East Coast. For a five-room bungalow, clean and bright, across the street from Hollenbeck Park, she paid $28 a month. For Seema, arriving wearily from her nine-month ordeal on the road, her mother's house was home.

Tama and Al arrived from Seattle, and Al went back to New York to report on his teaching experience. He wrote that the crates they had left behind had vanished, along with the people who had promised to send them on. As well as clothes and linens, they lost family treasures from England and Russia, and Seema lost the book of photos and poems her English boyfriend had made for her.

In Los Angeles, Jim went out looking for work painting houses, and Tama and Seema went to the needle trades district, the only place, they were told, where women could find jobs.

The sisters each had a dime for carfare as they set out in the morning to look for work. The trolley that took them across the bridge from Boyle Heights to downtown Los Angeles cost a nickel. They carefully stowed their nickel change in their pockets and trudged around the garment factories, looking for signs that said, HELP WANTED. There were very few of those, and they were all looking for people with experience.

At the end of the day they debated with each other whether to spend their remaining nickels on a trolley, or buy cream puffs and walk home. They both loved whipped cream.

As they walked across the bridge, eating their cream puffs, they discussed their strategy for the next day. They would say they had lots of experience, they decided, and they would mention several of the places where they had unsuccessfully applied for work already.

Sure enough, the next day they were both hired as finishers. In the large room where they worked, men with great shears stood and cut many layers of material, up to an inch thick, with patterns pinned on top. They handed the pieces on to women who sat at electric sewing machines. Once the women stitched the pieces together into garments, they gave them to the finishers, whose job was to cut loose threads and trim the seams before the garments were handed on to others who cut and stitched the buttonholes. Most of the workers were immigrant women from Europe, whose husbands were unable to find jobs; these women were the sole wage earners for their families.

Tama had worked as a milliner, and she had also done a lot of sewing for the family, so she was comfortable with the work, but Seema was awkward and slow. She watched the other finishers wielding their scissors, holding them close to the blades, but she couldn't get her fingers to work like theirs. The foreman who had hired the sisters hovered nearby, watching.

At the end of the second day Seema said to Tama, "Look, if you want this job, I'd better leave, otherwise we'll both get fired. I just can't keep up." It was piecework, and they used the fastest workers to set the pace. The slowest ones were fired.

Seema was developing a clear sense of herself as a woman of the working class. Decades later, when she was pointed out as the fastest worker in a Hollywood motion picture lab, she would deliberately slow down, accommodating her pace to the needs of other workers.

After leaving the garment factory, she kept checking the papers until she found an advertisement for a job in a photofinishing lab, Winstead

Brothers in Long Beach. She was nervous as she sat in the train, rehearsing to herself her photofinishing experience. She couldn't remember the name of the lab where she had worked in Boston, and it was an important lab, one they would be sure to recognize, she thought.

But Mr. Winstead, a stocky, middle-aged man with a bit of a leer, wasn't interested in her resume. He asked her to show him what she could do in the darkroom, and she did. She had learned a lot at her previous jobs. Then he interviewed her. The interview, conducted in his office, was sprinkled with off-color jokes, and she saw him watching her reactions. In self-defense, she chose not to react at all.

When she started working in the darkroom developing prints, he came in behind her and casually put his hands on her shoulders, letting them start to travel down toward her breasts. She invariably moved away, and when he made remarks she coolly changed the subject. Eventually he stopped bothering her. But her friend Jackie, a shy young mother whose nerve did not match her height of six feet, had a harder time fending off his advances.

"I don't know what to do when he comes after me in the darkroom," she said to Seema.

"I'll tell you what," Seema said. "I'll keep an eye out, and when I see him going toward you, I'll come over too."

And she did. She would find an excuse to walk over to Jackie's place in the dim, yellow-green light, and she would hover there until Mr. Winstead left. The two women joked about little Seema protecting big Jackie.

One day Mr. Winstead hired an attractive young blonde woman to work in the darkroom. At the end of the day she went into his office, leaving the door wide open.

"I want you to know," she said, in a clear, penetrating voice, "that if I were looking for sex I wouldn't come to you for it, and if you are looking for sex with me, you are sadly mistaken, as I came here to work. Now please give me my wages for today. I am leaving."

Mr. Winstead didn't come out of his office for hours, and the women were delighted. Most of them were afraid to rebuff him for fear of losing their jobs; one woman had already left when she became pregnant by him.

Tama worked in the garment factory until Al returned and found a job as an accountant in the oil fields at Signal Hill, near Long Beach, where they rented a one-room cottage on Cherry Avenue. When Tama got pregnant they found a new, fully furnished two-bedroom house on Platt Street that had been repossessed by the bank. It was the nicest house Tama had lived in since England.

Reva met Sam Berson at a New Year's Eve benefit dance for *Freiheit,* the Yiddish Communist daily paper. Sam was a grocer who courted Reva and told her that he would support her, so she wouldn't have to work so hard. His son Frank came to live with them, then Freda joined them, having ended her relationship with Brownie soon after they moved out West from New York. Freda and Frank drifted together, and eventually they married. For several years they continued to live with Reva and Sam.

Working at Winstead Brothers, Seema had an hour's commute to Long Beach on the Red Train. She loved the trip, as it gave her precious time to herself: she could read, knit or just gaze out the window. She and Jim had rented a flat of their own in Los Angeles. Jim was finding occasional work, and when Seema was free she went along and helped. She liked hanging wallpaper, as it required some measurement and calculation, reminding her of mathematics in school. Jim was also doing movement work, writing, making speeches at rallies, working with young people as he had done in Boston.

She and Jim shared work and a bed, but there was neither sex nor intimacy between them. She knew by now that she wanted more than camaraderie, and she had begun to suspect that she might even enjoy sex with someone other than Jim.

A photo from that period of Seema in painters' overalls has a twenty-first century feeling—her wild curly hair is combed up on top of her head, her hands jammed into the overalls; she looks slim, cool, aloof (fig. 13). Perhaps nothing much has changed in the world since that picture was taken, around 1930. Or is it Seema, transcending her time?

Jim hung onto their marriage through the years of sexual rebuffs and coolness, hoping it would eventually work out. Seema stayed with him for five years, having no model for separation in her family history, and no pattern for talking things over with her mother or sisters. She had no pattern for discussing it with me either, so many years later, and at first she brushed my questions aside.

"I don't remember," she would say, her voice flat.

The atmosphere between her and Jim grew more and more uncomfortable. They never fought, but Seema began to spend her time after work in Long Beach, meeting Tama and Al's friends there. She met Stirling Alexander, a young intellectual who confessed to her that he had tuberculosis and probably wouldn't live much longer. She also met Stirling's friend Clarence Lingeman. Seema was attracted to Stirling, a lovely, thoughtful man, but she also liked Clarence's kind, joking ways.

One evening when Seema came home from Long Beach, Jim was in the kitchen. Was he cooking dinner for them, or was he getting a beer from the icebox?

She blurted out what she had been thinking for a long while, "It's not working, Jim. I want to leave."

Tears rolled down his face. This was the first time she had seen him cry.

"Don't you think we could try again?"

"It's no use. We've been together five years now and it hasn't worked. It's over."

They stood facing each other, awkward. The kitchen was not cozy, Seema thought. It was another bare, rented flat, not a home. She hadn't the heart to make a home with Jim.

LONG BEACH

On a spring morning in 1930 Seema lay in bed, enjoying the feeling of her body next to Clarence's. The first time they'd made love, Clarence had been surprised by her shyness, not what he'd expected from a married woman. Once he realized that she was genuinely timid and inexperienced he had drawn her to him, initiating her into the pleasures of sex with a sensitive partner.

It was Sunday and they were sleeping in at her place, the first she'd had on her own, a studio in Long Beach close to the ocean, where she

figure 14. Seema and Clarence Lingeman,
ca. 1930. Courtesy of Seema Weatherwax.

often went for a dip before or after work. She had never learned to swim, but she would paddle out on a board, lying on her stomach, then ride the gentle waves in to shore.

She and Clarence had drifted together without volition on her part. She hadn't said anything to her family about her new relationship, waiting to see how it would develop.

There was a knock at the door. Seema said, "Come in," thinking it was their friend Stirling. But Frank, Freda's husband, stood in the doorway, looking from Seema to Clarence, as they sat up in bed.

"Oh! I'm sorry. We were just wondering what happened to you—we're all waiting." He backed out, muttering something indistinct. Seema and Clarence looked at each other and giggled.

At Tama and Al's house, where the family was gathered for Sunday lunch, Seema arrived late, apologizing. Frank had of course reported his discovery to the others, who were surprised because they thought Seema was attracted to Clarence's friend Stirling, but they all liked Clarence and were ready to accept him into the family.

He was six feet tall, handsome, good-tempered, and capable, with a generous sense of humor, skilled at building work, always able to earn a good living. He was raised German Catholic in Missouri, speaking Low German (Platt Deutsch), which was so similar to Yiddish that he and Reva could chat together. They became fast friends, and Tama looked up to him as an older brother. But Seema was not in love with him.

Tama had just had her baby, Joy. Clarence loved Joy and he integrated himself into the family. He was very good in every way, and I discovered what sex was with him, but I still didn't feel, what shall I say? I was glad to be with him in that period, but there were some problems. He was ten years older, and I was still young for my age. I hadn't really developed, emotionally. There was a big gap between us. He had been everywhere, he had done everything, and he was ready to settle down.

Meanwhile the country was in the grip of depression. In 1930 there were five million unemployed; by 1932 that figure would rise to thirteen million.

Clarence finished changing Joy's diaper and sat her expertly on his knee, bouncing her a little, which made her laugh. They were babysitting for

Tama and Al, and Seema was always happy to let Clarence take care of the diapers.

"I'd like you to see Tahiti, Seema. It's the most beautiful place in the world, and I know you'll love it."

"Okay," she said. "I'm game to try."

After a stint in the army, Clarence spent some years at sea as a merchant sailor. He fell in love with French Polynesia and bought some property in Moorea, an island near Tahiti. Now he wanted to settle there with Seema. For Seema, reading books and looking at pictures of Tahiti, it was a new adventure.

She had become pregnant a few months earlier, shortly after she and Clarence had started living together, and she had thought she would like to have a baby, but one day she started spotting, then bleeding heavily. She panicked, fearing that the baby would be abnormal, not realizing that she was miscarrying.

My friend Doris was very sophisticated and she knew all the ropes, I thought.

She said, "You'd better go and have yourself cleaned out," and the only place she could think of was an abortion doctor.

At that time contraceptives were illegal and abortions were not to be thought about. If you even thought about an abortion, you were in jail, it seemed.

So I went through the horrors of an illegal abortion—darkness, you can't cry out no matter how much pain you have, you have to keep your mouth shut, and you leave there immediately afterward. I came home, and the next day I couldn't walk without holding on to things, my legs were stiff, and I realized I was getting blood poisoning. So I thought, "This time I'm not going to ask anybody," and I went to a reputable doctor. He scolded me—he said there was no need for me to go to an abortionist, but I didn't know that. He cleaned me out and asked me if I knew the name of the doctor who had done the abortion, but I didn't.

Seema did not tell anyone what had happened, not Clarence, not her sisters nor Reva. Now she was feeling restless, unsure what she wanted to do next, so she welcomed the idea of going to Tahiti.

Clarence went over ahead of her, planning to build a simple house on his Moorea property before Seema arrived. She applied for a visa from the French consulate, as Tahiti was a colony of France. She had no legal citizenship—her birthplace was Czarist Russia, which had since become the USSR—and the French officials told her to have her papers from Russia notarized. The notary didn't speak or read Russian so Seema translated the papers for him, thinking to herself, "I could tell him I am the Czar's daughter—he wouldn't know the difference!"

Obtaining the visa took a month, then she set off on a ship bound for Tahiti, with two hundred dollars she had saved from her work at Winstead Brothers. Her friends and family were worried about her rashness, leaving a good job in the midst of the Depression, but she was optimistic as she said good-bye to them.

I said, "You've got to take a chance." Clarence and I had been together for about a year at that time. He wanted me to go with him, and it sounded very exciting.

A pattern of adventure was emerging in Seema's life, separate from her family life of parties and political activity. She had come with her family from Russia to England to Boston, New Jersey and California; now she was heading further west.

таніті

The ship entered the harbor of Papeete at sunrise on July 14, 1931. Nothing she had heard or read prepared Seema for her first sight of Tahiti. The harbor water shimmered in the early light in shades of turquoise, green and blue, and huge palm trees fringed the shore, with green mountains rising in the background, everything painted fresh by the morning sun. A light breeze blew as they docked, stirring the soft, warm air.

She had enjoyed herself hugely on the crossing from California, dancing every night, as she and Tama had done eight years earlier when they crossed the Atlantic. Many of the officers and passengers became friends and they invited her to join them on a sightseeing party when

figure 15. Mariposa Cafe, Papeete, photo by Seema Weatherwax, ca. 1932. Courtesy of Seema Weatherwax.

they landed. But she was anxious to send a telegram to Clarence and find her way to Moorea. Once through customs she saw an old taxicab idling at the roadside.

"I'd like to go to the Marseilles Hotel." She had found the name in her guidebook.

The driver didn't budge. She repeated the name of the hotel, thinking he had not understood her. Still nothing.

Finally, "I can't take you there, Mademoiselle."

"But why not?"

"Because—" he still hesitated, "it is now a brothel."

"Oh."

She paused to digest this information, then said, in a small voice, "Can you recommend a place?"

There commenced a long, desultory tour of Papeete, with many stops along the main road to consult with friends of the driver and ask where a room might be found. The ship was in with its cargo from the mainland and it was Bastille Day weekend—the town was jammed with people from the neighbor islands.

Finally, the taxi pulled up to a ramshackle building on a back street not far from the center of town, near their original starting point. It was a seedy little place: an open gutter ran in the street outside, smelling of garbage and urine; inside cockroaches and spiders scuttled into corners; the bedsheets were gray; the shower hadn't been cleaned in years. However, nothing else was available. Seema agreed to stay and turned to pay the driver, but the fare he demanded was exorbitant, outrageous, she thought, for such a short distance, especially as he had been gossiping with his cronies most of the time. She objected, he argued, and Seema felt frustrated with her lack of French or Tahitian.

Just then some of the French officers from the ship appeared and they came to the defense of their favorite "Mademoiselle Sophie," arguing the driver down to a more reasonable fare.

Seema asked where she could find a telephone but was told there was no way of reaching Moorea except by boat. She had no idea of how to contact Clarence. She left her bags in her grimy room and walked into town, to the harbor, where she found an outdoor cafe and ordered a drink. As she sipped her drink she felt some tears slipping down her cheeks.

"Can I help you?" The woman was very beautiful, Polynesian, Seema thought. She wore a Western-style dress and she spoke English fluently. She listened sympathetically to Seema's tale.

"I'll stay with you until we find a way to contact your friend," she said. Relieved, Seema looked at her surroundings for the first time, realizing that the cafe was on the waterfront, overlooking the harbor and the boats that came and went. Honey-yellow hibiscus flowers opened their papery petals, and the covered porch where she sat at a square wooden table was lined with palm trees growing in oil drums. This was the Mariposa Cafe and Hotel, with a wooden sign on the wall advertising Accommodations for Tourists, and Coffee and Tea Served with Meals, as well as various drinks and sundries.

The two women chatted until they saw a boat coming into the harbor, a small schooner.

"That's the boat from Moorea. Why don't you ask the captain to take a message to your friend?"

Seema ran down to the landing, and as the boat pulled in she saw Clarence, ready to disembark. At the sight of his familiar, kind face she was ready again for adventure, ready to deal with grimy sheets and a dirty shower.

The next day the big ship left and they were able to get a room at the Mariposa. They stayed on for the Bastille Day celebrations, which lasted several days, shopping and seeing the sights. Papeete was a small town with wooden buildings, one story high—the largest were the Yacht Club and the government building. The Mariposa Hotel, the post office, and the harbor building were all on the waterfront, and on the back streets were Chinese restaurants and shops, shoemakers who made custom sandals, and dressmakers who sewed made-to-order outfits from hand-blocked cotton cloth.

Clarence took her to the public market early in the morning, where fresh fruits and flowers, vegetables, and fish were displayed for sale. According to local custom, Seema was constantly offered flower leis— her favorite were made from the small, fragrant white flowers they called *tiare Tahiti*, that smelled like gardenias.

When they took the island schooner to Moorea, the eleven-mile crossing lasted several hours, laden as the small boat was with people, cows, pigs, and cages of chickens and ducks, all on deck and many of them seasick. The oily smell of the engine dominated the pungent atmosphere. They left the lagoon outside Papeete, entering the open sea; then the small island of Moorea appeared, lushly green, sparsely settled, its mountains rising from the center. Seema and Clarence stopped in at the small store at the pier where they landed and arranged to rent a mule for her luggage, then they walked two miles up the mountain along a forest trail. Moorea was much wilder than Tahiti, more like what she had imagined.

moorea

Their house was very different from the open structures with thatched roofs and wooden floors she had seen elsewhere. Clarence had built a wooden roof as well as a wood floor, and he'd covered the open sides of

figure 16. Moorea, photo by Seema Weatherwax, 1931.
Courtesy of Seema Weatherwax.

the house with wire mesh. It was not so picturesque as the other dwellings, but Seema soon came to appreciate the protection from mosquitoes, other insects, and rats, which were abundant in the tropical forest. Two wooden steps took her into the one large room where they would sleep, cook, and eat. A large bed was spread with a quilt that Clarence's grandmother had made.

He showed her around proudly. He had built an outhouse, and he was in the process of piping in water from a nearby stream so they would have a faucet on the outside of the house with fresh running water. He had already started a garden with vegetables and fruit, still very small, but soon they would eat from it. Meanwhile, there were bananas, avocados, and oranges growing nearby in the forest; breadfruit, taro, mangoes, coconuts, pineapple, and papayas were easily found. They bought rice and duck eggs from the Chinese farmers who lived down below, and every few days, people came up the trail with fish to sell. Bread, meat, and other staples were sold at the country store down at the pier.

I was young and used to the outdoors from our time in England. When we lived in Moorea I thought nothing of running down the two miles to the little store for a loaf of bread or a pack of cigarettes.

At first Seema was enchanted with their way of life. It was like summer camp near Boston, like her childhood memories of picking fruit and berries in Chernigov. In their wooden house she and Clarence kept three bunches of bananas hanging from the rafters, one green, one ripening, and one ready to eat. When they finished a bunch, they would go into the forest to pick another green bunch, and they would also pick sacks full of wild oranges, which they then brought home on a mule.

Clarence built a wooden bridge across the little stream near their house and Seema caught shrimp from the stream and cooked them. She learned how to prepare breadfruit and tarot, waiting until the tarot reached a certain ripeness, then boiling and mashing it to resemble mashed potatoes, which she craved. But there was no sour cream in the islands, and she missed that more than anything else from home. She laughed, remembering how, in this tropical paradise, she had·tried to re-create the flavors of her Russian Jewish home.

Once a month the boat brought mail from the mainland, and Seema had letters from her family. They were struggling in the Depression— Reva wrote that Sam had lost his grocery stores and Freda and Frank were selling peanuts on the street, but they were never able to earn back the cost of the peanuts. Reva was supporting them all with her work for Robinson's department store. Al and Tama were fine, and they reported with delight on Joy's achievements as a toddler.

Seema responded with stories about getting settled in Moorea and about their neighbors, an Englishman and his Tahitian companion. John Farnham was a remittance man who had the property next to theirs. In England, Seema explained, when upper-class people had several sons, the eldest inherited the property and the youngest went off to foreign lands. Their families sent money every month, remittances, to live on comfortably so they didn't have to work. She was amused, like an anthropologist noting strange customs of the idle class.

Seema became friendly with the Tahitian woman who was John Farnham's partner. He didn't deserve her, Seema thought. He was a typical upper-class Englishman, useless and arrogant. He wanted to turn his property into a sort of wild animal preserve, but all he had were some chickens that he'd let loose in the forest and a few wild boars.

figure 17. Seema and friend, Tahiti, ca. 1932.
Courtesy of Seema Weatherwax.

Seema didn't care for John, but he was their nearest neighbor, so the two couples often got together. Her Tahitian friend showed Seema how to tie the *pareo*, a traditional garment consisting of a length of hand-printed cloth, wrapped around the torso, leaving arms, shoulders, and legs bare, and the two women walked together down the trail to the coral reefs where you could watch fantastically colored fish swimming in the clear water.

Clarence was content in his island paradise with Seema, cultivating his garden and working on the house. He grew coffee, showing Seema how to remove first the hard outer shell, then the inner shell, finally roasting and grinding the beans. He had many skills, having worked as a soldier, a sailor, a butcher, and a carpenter; whatever he turned his hand to flourished. Often Seema came up the trail from the harbor to find that he had put out all the furniture and was giving the house a thorough cleaning.

Seema was not interested in gardening or building; she was a competent housekeeper and cook, but this did not satisfy her. Her life on Moorea was an extended vacation: she and Clarence went to luaus where whole suckling pigs were roasted in fire pits in the ground with breadfruit and taro, and their Tahitian friends danced hula; they sat on their porch sipping drinks with the Farnhams; once a week they went into the forest to gather bananas and oranges. After five months in Moorea, the charm of her life there began to fade. She had started to take photographs of people and scenes on Moorea, and she was frustrated at not being able to develop them herself.

Once in a while she and Clarence went over to Tahiti on the little schooner with its load of copra (fresh coconut fiber) spread out to dry on the decks. They stayed at the Mariposa, on the main street overlooking the waterfront, where Seema had sat crying on her first day. This was the only real hotel in Tahiti, owned by an amiable Frenchman.

One day they were sitting in the large front room of the cafe and Seema noticed some cameras in one of the smaller rooms in the back. She discovered that the Frenchman had once been a photographer. She was welcome, he said, to look at what he had back there.

There was a pile of photographic equipment, most of what was needed for developing film and making contact prints. Seema started to hatch a plan to deal with her photographs and her boredom. She was able to come to an arrangement with the owner, drawing on her high-school French, as he spoke no English. She rented the room with its equipment, and she started a photofinishing and portrait business, the only one in Tahiti at that time. She also rented one of the hotel rooms over the cafe, where she lived for the next seven months.

There was no enlarger, but when she described what was needed to Clarence, he converted one of the cameras into an enlarger for her, using a condenser lens and a camera bellows that they found among the Frenchman's equipment. She had done very little enlarging, which entailed separating the negative from the paper rather than making a contact print, but she knew enough to be able to figure the process out for herself, experimenting with timing as she went.

She had to apply for a business permit from the local authorities, who did not usually issue permits to foreigners. The government officials were charmed by her, and they readily granted a permit.

And so she became known in Tahiti as Mademoiselle Sophie, the attractive young woman who ran her own photo business. When a Hollywood movie crew came to the island to make *Mr. Robinson Crusoe*, starring Douglas Fairbanks, Sr., she developed their publicity photographs.

She spoke of this time in her life matter-of-factly, unimpressed by her own creative and entrepreneurial abilities.

In Tahiti, for the first time, she tried her hand at taking photographs for her own pleasure. Working with a simple box camera, one of the folding models from Eastman Kodak, she photographed the sea, the trees, and the people of Tahiti, experimenting with the use of natural light, trying to capture the feeling of the islands in shades of black-and-white. She could not capture the wild colors of the fish, nor the vivid colors of the sky and flowers, so she concentrated instead on shapes and contrasts and on what she could do in the darkroom, beginning the work she would continue later in Yosemite.

Clarence was supportive, helping her to set up the darkroom, coming over frequently on the little schooner to visit, but Seema didn't go back to Moorea. She had, for the first time in her life, become seasick on the little schooner with its smells of coconut, diesel, and animals and no bathroom facilities, and although she would have liked to revisit her former home, she found the trip, which often included a side excursion of several hours if fish were sighted, too much of an ordeal. Instead, she and Clarence explored Tahiti, getting to know the Chinese restaurants on the back streets of Papeete, riding bicycles outside the town to the other side of the island.

One time we decided to go round the island, which was like a big steep hill, with a cliff on one side and the ocean, way down below, on the other. We were riding along at breakneck speed, and I lost my pedals—they were spinning so fast. These were bikes with the brake on the pedal.

It could have been a second, or two seconds, or a minute, I don't know how long, but I thought that this was the end. I finally got my feet back in. I didn't even tell Clarence how bad it was, and he didn't realize, because he was ahead of me, but it was terrifying. It didn't stop me from running around on the bicycle, though.

Once or twice a day she bathed at the beach or in the lagoon. She loved the sun and her skin darkened easily. Snapshots from that period show her exotically beautiful, with flowers in her hair, her body wrapped in a brightly printed *pareo,* bare arms linked with one of her Tahitian women friends (fig. 17). There was a law at that time, thanks to the missionaries, that forbade anyone from wearing a *pareo* in town, but it was the standard dress for bathing.

It was rare to see a single foreign woman in Papeete, and Seema received frequent proposals of marriage from the men on the island—French, Portuguese, Americans, and some of the wealthier Tahitians—"And not just marriage, I also got a lot of sexual propositions," she said, emphatically. She ignored them all, feeling loyal to Clarence and absorbed in her adventure of running her own business, but she often went to parties with the woman she had met when she first arrived. They had a tacit understanding that when Seema said she had enough, it was time for them to leave the party together. Seema thought that her friend understood her commitment to Clarence.

One evening a wealthy Tahitian, who had been educated abroad and spoke English, invited Seema, her friend, and another man to drive about ten miles from the main town to a resort hotel, famous for its view and excellent food. They sat outside on the terrace with drinks, watching the palm trees darken against the sunset sky with its streaks and washes of orange, red, purple, and green; then the other couple walked away. They did not return, and when Seema asked about them, her companion told her they had left to go back to Papeete. As he refilled her glass with wine, she realized that he expected her to spend the night with him. Except for the waiters and hotel staff, they were alone in the hotel. There were no phones and no vehicle to take her back to town until the next morning, when the taxi would return.

Seema gathered herself together, sat up as tall as she could, and said firmly, using her best standard English, "I am known to the governor here, and all the people in office. If you attempt to do anything that I don't want, I will let them know what happened and you will be in big trouble."

She spent a miserable night, curled in a chair in the hotel dining room.

Later her friend apologized, saying she thought Seema understood that the hotel was well-known as the place to go for romantic trysts. She shrugged off Seema's protests. After all, why not enjoy oneself?

I had an unusual experience [in Papeete]. No other women and very few men had businesses there, because it was very hard to get permission from the French government. I lived there a whole year, so I got to know the Tahitian women as friends, not just as playthings of the tourists, white men who came there for a thrill.

RETURN

One restaurant in Papeete had a short-wave radio. The news was disturbing—in Germany Chancellor Bruening, the last defender of the Republic, had been forced to resign, and Hitler's power was on the rise. Seema wondered what she was doing out there in the tropics, partying, when so much was going on in the world. If war was declared, she worried, she might be stranded in Tahiti.

Her original three-month visa had been extended twice by the local authorities. Now she had to leave or else apply for French citizenship. If she chose the latter, she would lose her immigrant's standing in the

U.S., and she would have to reapply for admission on the quota system all over again, a process that could take years. She decided to return to California.

She told Clarence about her decision one night when they were eating at their favorite Chinese restaurant on one of the back streets of Papeete, a place where you entered through the kitchen. There were long counters with plates of chicken, fish, and vegetables, and you pointed at the food you wanted prepared for you.

"Why don't you stay here, Clarence? You love it in Moorea, more than anywhere!"

"If you leave, I'll go with you."

It was settled. Seema could not allow herself to see how much Clarence loved her. Even in the telling, so long afterward, she would not allow herself to dwell on this, or she would feel too much guilt, but what else could she have done? She thought it was a shame Clarence sold his beloved property on Moorea, but he didn't want to live there without her.

The restaurant that had the radio was also on a back street. It was the nicest restaurant in town, with white cloths and candles on each table. French businessmen and the wealthier tourists ate there, and Seema and Clarence went for special meals, as well as to listen to the radio. The news got worse, as Hitler's brown-shirted storm troopers marched in German city streets singing their Nazi song: "*Blut muss fliessen, Blut muss fliessen! Blut muss fliessen knueppelhageldick! Haut'se doch zusammen, haut'se doch zusammen! Diese gotverdammte Juden Republik!*" ("Blood must flow, Blood must flow from a thick hail of cudgels! Let's smash it up, let's smash it up! That goddamned Jewish republic!")

I asked Seema if she remembered any reactions among people in Tahiti to the news from Europe.

Most of the people I knew were not interested in political things of that sort. That's why they were there, to get away from it all. It didn't concern them. I was concerned, and Clarence was somewhat concerned, but he also was there to get away from it all.

Preparing to go home, Seema bought sandals and tropical cloth for her family. She and Clarence stayed until the day her visa expired, walking aboard their ship adorned with flower leis from their Tahitian friends, who had given several luaus in their honor. It was July 1932.

She returned to Los Angeles after thirteen months away, richer than when she left, with over five hundred dollars saved from her photographic business.

For me, it was all a big adventure. I didn't realize until we'd been there a while that Clarence wanted to stay. But I wasn't ready to settle down.

I fell in liking with Clarence, not in love—it was nothing like the passion I felt later. But I didn't know about that yet.

Clarence and I didn't discuss politics. We could tell where we stood, on what I call the right side, with the working class. He was for labor and for all the things that I was for, but we never sat down and had a political talk. We had no disagreements about anything, except that he wanted to live in Tahiti. He had thought of it as a retirement place, and I was not ready to go into hiding. It was pretty hard for him to accept that.

They went to stay with Tama and Al in Long Beach, where Seema returned to her old job at Winstead Brothers. Reva and Sam were still sharing an apartment with Freda and Frank in Los Angeles. Seema and Clarence had come back to a world that felt far from paradise.

In September of 1932 the German delegates walked out of the international Disarmament Conference. A few months later, Hitler became chancellor of Germany.

In the United States the effects of the Depression under Herbert Hoover's administration were creating desperation among the millions who were unemployed. Food rotted in the fields while people went hungry; banks were closing all over the country; over a million hoboes had taken to the roads and railroads; and talk of revolution was widespread. In November Franklin D. Roosevelt was elected president after a frantic campaign by the Republicans to retain office. The months before his inauguration were some of the bleakest in U.S. history, and in December there was a National Hunger March on Washington, filmed by the newly formed Film and Photo League.

earthquake

MARCH 10, 1933, 4:54 P.M. PST

Seema and Freda stood in the doorway of their mother's second-floor apartment, holding on to the doorframe as the earth fell apart beneath them. People always said you should stand in a doorway if there was an earthquake. Reva was running back and forth across the room, screaming, *"Meine kinde, meine kinde!"* as dishes fell from the cupboard all around her.

"Mama, mama, come here," they yelled.

Finally, Seema grabbed Reva as she ran past. Summoning all her courage ("For after all, who hits their own mother?") she slapped

figure 18. Reva, photo by Seema Weatherwax, ca. 1933. Courtesy of Seema Weatherwax.

Reva hard, on the cheek. Reva stared at her. Just then, the horrible shaking stopped.

The three women crouched in the doorway, consoling each other. It was quite a while before they could leave the building, because the staircase kept rippling from aftershocks. Once they were out, Reva calmed down, but she worried aloud about Tama and little Joy.

Seema was up from Long Beach visiting her mother and Freda. Clarence was at the Veterans' Hospital in San Diego, being treated for his old illness, amoebic dysentery from his time in the army. Sam and Frank were at work when the earthquake began, but they rushed home, and within two hours Al arrived with Tama and Joy from Long Beach. That night the family camped outside, along with many of their neighbors, afraid to stay indoors, and just before eleven, they felt a huge aftershock. More debris fell and several buildings that were still standing collapsed. Five more big shocks in the next twenty-four hours kept everyone outside, where they camped for the next two days and nights.

Seema discovered that Clarence's hospital had indeed been shaken by the quake, which reached all the way down to San Diego, but Clarence was all right and would soon rejoin them.

On the third day after the earthquake, Seema, Al, Tama, and Joy returned to Long Beach. Their house was full of broken crockery, and the piano had traveled from one end of the house to the other, but the damage was relatively minor. Seema went back to work at Winstead Brothers, summoning all her courage each time she had to climb the rickety wooden stairs. The aftershocks were to continue sporadically for three more years.

She took some photographs of damaged buildings, and as more earthquake film came through the lab to be processed, she asked if she could make copies of the photos she found interesting: a ruined church with a big sign on the front: "Rock of Ages"; a broken three-story building, with each story tilting in a different direction. In this way she created a photographic archive of the earthquake and its aftermath.

I went up three flights of stairs in a building that was condemned because of the earthquake, and I'd work at photofinishing during the day.

I'd shake every once in a while and come down the shaky stairs and go home. That's what you did, you had to work.

Unemployment had reached an all-time high, with thirteen to fourteen million Americans out of work. Everywhere there were breadlines, and shanty towns sprang up across the country.

DEATH

Seema and Clarence stood at the checkout counter in the grocery store, waiting to unload two grocery carts piled high with food for a party. Seema's birthday was August 25, and Freda's was August 30, so they usually celebrated together, with all the family and many friends.

We were a partying family. We'd celebrate at the drop of a hat, just to have an excuse to get together.

Tama was at home in the Long Beach house they all shared, with Joy, who was napping.

Two policemen came up to Seema. "Are you Tama Smith's sister?"

She knew immediately that something had happened. Instead of joking about her obvious resemblance to Tama, she simply stood there, staring at them.

"What is it?" Clarence said.

Al was dead. Driving home from work, he was struck head-on by a drunk driver, who also died in the collision. Both men left wives and small children. Two of Al's co-workers had gone to the house to tell Tama, who started to scream and flail about until she was held down and sedated.

Two neighborhood girls from a Christian family who used to babysit Joy came over and took the four-year-old home with them. The girls told Joy that Al had gone to Heaven and she came back the next day expecting to see her father returned from his visit.

The family gathered around Tama. She and Al had loved each other deeply, and Al was a family favorite, like Clarence, good-natured and kind, an enthusiastic, gifted, radical teacher. No one knew what to say. Reva, who had stood by when Tama gave birth to Joy, encouraging her

figure 19. Joy, Clarence, Seema, Tama, Al, Long Beach,
ca. 1934. Courtesy of Seema Weatherwax.

to scream when the pains came, now sat close to her youngest daughter, saying nothing at all. Seema did not cry; she felt the death of her brother-in-law as a great weight inside her chest.

There was a lot to decide. An insurance agent came to the house with a check for two thousand dollars made out to Tama. Each time Al had mentioned taking out insurance, Tama had cried and said she didn't want to think about it, so without telling her he had bought a double indemnity policy. At first Tama refused to take the check, but Seema and Freda convinced her that she needed the money, for Joy as well as for herself.

Al's family wanted Tama to come to New York with Joy. She booked passage on a boat that went through the Panama Canal, around Cape Hatteras, and Seema and Clarence helped her to pack up the house in Long Beach. They were all anxious to leave the place that had once been so lively.

Mr. Ward, a man Seema knew at Winstead Brothers, left to start a new photo lab in Los Angeles and offered her a job. She and Clarence rented an apartment, and Seema worked for Mr. Ward until she realized that he was looking to her for the comfort he wasn't finding in his marriage.

He was Catholic, married to this woman who was completely engrossed in Catholic works. Every time he came home she was off again, and they had no life at all together. So he fell in love with me. He never said a word about it, but I would sit down at my printer and he would rush over and put a pillow behind my back, or he would come over and say, "Would you like a cup of tea?"

I realized it was not a boss and worker relationship, or even an ordinary friendship. He was showing that he needed something, and because he was Catholic, and because he was a decent guy, he never said anything. So after a while I just gave my notice.

She found another job that combined selling cameras and working in a darkroom. One afternoon the manager asked her to come into the back and help him test out a new lens by posing for him. That was fine until he asked her to take off her blouse and drape a piece of tulle around herself. By now, Seema's way of dealing with this kind of harassment was decisive—she left. She had excellent references and skills; and she had no trouble finding a job in another photo lab.

When she heard that a branch of the Film and Photo League was forming in Los Angeles, she was eager to join. Similar groups had already formed in New York and Chicago, composed of photographers and filmmakers who were documenting events of the time from a radical perspective.

At first Seema helped to organize shows of League members' work, and later she helped with subtitling and arranging screenings of films that came in from the Spanish Civil War. The Spanish films were used to rally support for the International Brigade, which fought alongside the Spanish loyalists against Franco and his fascist rebels.

These were heady times for those who believed, as Seema did, that humanity could attain a better, more just way of living together. In 1934 American Communists began organizing in cooperation with other left-wing groups such as the Popular Front. Party discipline ensured that progressives all over the country worked on the same issue at the same time, so that enormous force was brought to bear on each issue, contributing to a sense of effective solidarity on the Left.

It was a time when photographers were going into the fields to document farmworkers' struggles and filmmakers were making newsreels about strikes and demonstrations, and everyone thought they were saving the world for the working class.

Clarence was not a joiner. He accompanied Seema to benefit dances, parties, and meetings, and he agreed easily with her views about the need for racial justice and justice for working people, but they never discussed politics. She felt, increasingly, that something was missing in their relationship.

There was a restlessness in me. I was still trying to find a man on a white horse, someone who meant more to me. Clarence wasn't helping me to grow emotionally.

foLLowiNG Heart aND body

Seema was alone, and she did not like it. She looked around at her rented one-room flat, then she sat down to write a letter to Clarence, who was off in the desert, working on the great aqueduct that would bring water to Los Angeles.

In 1934 Southern California had emerged from the worst drought of the century with a sweeping plan to bring water into the Central Valley by means of giant aqueducts and dams. Congress and President Roosevelt decided to put money into the project, which would transform the valley and Los Angeles. When Clarence had a chance to work on the aqueduct, he was excited by the challenge and the money to be earned.

"It will be hard work, but I can earn a lot," he told Seema. "Then, after a couple of years, we'll be free to travel, to do what we like."

Seema was not impressed with his plan. She wanted him at home with her.

"I won't stay at home waiting for you, Clarence," she told him. "I need to have companionship now. This is not a good time for me."

But Clarence did not seem to hear her.

Seema was preparing to break with Clarence, though she was unwilling to acknowledge this even to herself. He was only ten years older, but she looked to him as a kind, fatherly figure rather than as a lover. Her restless mind and body sought a deeper partnership than she was finding with Clarence, but she hesitated to cause him pain. She was grateful to him for having awakened her to the pleasures of sex, and, after all, he had given up his wonderful property in Moorea to come back to California with her. Also, he had become a member of the family.

However, he would not listen to her. This became Seema's justification to herself for beginning to date other men, for she never discussed her decision with anyone else. When she went to Tahiti to set up her photographic business, she argued to herself, she had consulted Clarence, and he had agreed. But she had not agreed to his decision to go off for long stretches of time on the aqueduct. Very well then, she decided, if he was to be independent, so would she.

She started going out for dinner with male friends, going to benefits and meetings and dancing with anyone who asked her. As in Tahiti, she held back from forming intimate attachments with these men. She had not been sexual with any other man while she was still with Jim, and she would not do so while she was still loyal to Clarence. He came home every couple of weeks, just as he had come to Tahiti every couple of weeks to visit her from Moorea, calling or writing to let her know when he would arrive.

Tama wrote that she was returning from New York with Joy. Reva, Sam, Freda, Frank, Seema, and Clarence rented a four-bedroom house together, in order to have a place for Tama and Joy. Seema felt comfortable there, surrounded by family and friends. But the house didn't work out—there was a saloon next door and drunks wandered into their yard on weekend nights. After a few months they all found separate places again. Seema and Clarence rented another one-room flat, and Clarence kept on with his work on the aqueduct.

Seema's letter to Clarence stressed how serious she was about not wanting to be alone. She wanted him to leave his job on the aqueduct, and she wanted him to let her know his answer immediately. When he did not reply, she decided that he must have given up on her, and that he was not planning to return. It was at that point that she gave up on him. When an attractive young man came up to her at a meeting and asked if she would like to go out for a coffee afterward, she agreed.

She had met him before, this young African-American student, slim with dark brown skin, curly hair, and chiseled features. He was very bright and interested in progressive politics. They talked until late that first night and made another date; then it seemed easy and natural to invite him home. He was affectionate and then passionate, and Seema felt free with him.

They began to spend a lot of time together.

There were very few places we could go. It was impossible to go to a restaurant together. We would go to somebody's house, but we would not be able to go openly to a restaurant, because we were a mixed couple. Even in the black community I was not looked upon with favor.

Her young partner embarrassed Seema by kissing and fondling her in front of other people, and she preferred having him come over to the flat where they could be alone. He would bring his books with him and he impressed her with his ability to concentrate, whether she was playing music or talking to friends. Just so, she remembered, she had concentrated on her homework as a schoolgirl in England, surrounded by the uproar of the family.

They had intense discussions about racial issues, whether, for instance, mixed couples should have children, which was being hotly debated in progressive circles of the time, as their generation was starting to intermarry. Seema thought it placed an unfair burden on the children, an opinion she would change later when she got to know many mixed families. He was young and intent on his studies, not interested in becoming a father.

They were asleep the night Clarence came back from the aqueduct, three weeks after his last visit. Both of them sat up in bed, startled first by the noise of the door opening, and then by Clarence's shout of surprise when he realized Seema was not alone. He had been doing heavy work, and his muscles were strong. He grabbed the slim young man by his shoulders and pulled back his fist for a punch, but he couldn't bring himself to carry through, contenting himself instead with pushing him around, threatening him incoherently. As soon as Clarence let go of him, the terrified young man grabbed his clothes and left.

Seema pulled on slacks and a sweater and said in a low voice, "It's over now, Clarence. Will you take me to my mother's?"

Clarence nodded. He was silent on the way, and so was she.

Seema called her friend the next day to say they had better not meet again. He said he understood. She said goodbye to Clarence, saying she had tried to tell him how it was with her. He didn't respond. Seema thought he was stunned, having finally realized that their relationship was over. Soon he returned to the aqueduct and Seema started looking for another apartment. When Clarence came back to town he stayed with Tama and Joy. He kept close ties with Tama and the rest of the family until his death many years later, but Seema always avoided seeing him.

That was the only time in my life that I was not sure whether I wanted to live or die. I was ashamed that I had hurt him. He didn't deserve to be hurt. But by then I no longer expected him to come back. It wasn't a conscious, evil act on my part.

I never told a soul. Mother never asked why I came home in the middle of the night. That's the way our family was. We were close—if anyone needed anything, we would rally.

If Tama had a problem, she would tell us about it. Freda and I never did. Mother never spoke about her feelings about Father, or about Sam. We never spoke about things that were personal while we were living them.

I was never analytical. I just followed where my heart and my body wanted to go.

THIS MAN CHAN

Seema sat on the bench under the old fruit tree admiring her handiwork, a trellis covered with a climbing vine beside the little pond. "Not bad," she thought, remembering what the place had looked like when she'd first arrived. Edward Chandler Weston, who preferred to be called Chan, lived in a one-room house on the outskirts of Glendale. He kept his person and his darkroom clean and well-ordered but his small house was grubby; haphazard piles of paper, photographs, and books were stacked in every corner, and the yard was badly overgrown. After Seema moved in with Chan, her family and friends pitched in to help her transform the place, throwing out old magazines, scrubbing the kitchen and bath, and painting the walls so that everything was fresh and clean.

She was in love, with a strength of feeling that surprised her. She had first met Chan at the Film and Photo League.

He spoke softly, to the point, and he seemed like a nice guy that I'd like to know more. He asked if he could come to see me. I said yes, and when he came over, there were waves of magnetism. We just sat and talked and I felt almost compelled to embrace him, only I didn't. I had to restrain myself. It was a very quick sort of combustion.

Was it their second or the third date when they fell into bed? Seema could not remember, nor where they were, nor where she was living at the time, only that she felt a great need to be with him. Chan transformed her sense of what an intimate relationship could be.

It wasn't just a matter of him giving pleasure to me, but it was a mutual giving and sharing between us. Even though I'd enjoyed my relationship with Clarence, I never had this extreme passionate urge toward him as I had toward this man Chan.

figure 20. Chan Weston and Seema, Yosemite, ca. 1938. Courtesy of Seema Weatherwax.

She had not been ready to jump into living together with Chan when she first met him, soon after the breakup with Clarence. A friend told her about a small house for rent, at the end of Echo Park Avenue where the hills started. The house was built around an old oak tree that emerged from the roof as if it had grown there overnight.

Chan stayed often with Seema in her tree house on the hill, with its fireplace on one side of the main room and the living tree growing through the middle. In springtime the hillside was orange with nasturtiums, pungent with their spicy smell. But the lease expired after six months, and she rented a room in town. It was a large, light room with a private bath and entrance, but that didn't work out either—the couple she rented from disapproved of Chan's overnight visits.

They said their thirteen-year-old daughter would be corrupted, but I'm sure she knew more about sex than they did!

So Seema finally decided to move in with Chan. His young son, Ted, who was four when Seema and Chan first met, spent most weekends with them. He was the same age as Tama's daughter Joy and the two children often played together. Seema's family accepted Chan as they had accepted Jim at first, and Clarence forever. She knew that her mother was puzzled about why she had broken with Clarence, but Reva kept silent on the subject, as did Freda and Tama.

Chan loved photography and radical politics, and he and Seema talked eagerly together about the Film and Photo League, about Chan's work with the League photographing farmworkers, and about Seema's work helping to get subtitles made for films coming from the war in Spain.

For American radicals like Seema and Chan, the fight to defend the Spanish Republic against Franco's fascist rebels in Spain had a strong emotional appeal. Franco was supported by Hitler, whose forces were gathering strength in Europe, and when the Soviet Union lent support to the Spanish loyalists, American communists and progressives eagerly followed suit, organizing and raising money for the Abraham Lincoln Battalion and other volunteer forces that went to join the International Brigades fighting in Spain in 1937–38. Ernest Hemingway went to Spain and wrote the script for *The Spanish Earth*, a stirring documentary film about the war directed by the great Dutch filmmaker Joris Ivens—as soon as they got a print, the Film and Photo League organized many benefit screenings.

We were showing films all over Los Angeles . . . our projectionists went to big halls like the Embassy and we showed films about the civil war.

We were also taking photographs in Salinas [California] in the fields where they were trying to organize for better conditions and where there was a law called the criminal syndicalism law. There were many people who were imprisoned because they went out to the fields and talked to the

strikers. If three people met it was already considered a conspiracy. So,
many people went to jail. Well, people from the Film and Photo League
went out and photographed these things and Chan was one of the people
who went. I had a full-time job so I wasn't able to do much of that.

Chan's house was on property that had once belonged to his
mother's family. The Chandlers, for whom he was named, had owned
all the property in the neighborhood, now called Glendale, a suburb of
Los Angeles. Socialist-minded Chan hated to admit he came from such
a wealthy and conservative family (they owned the Los Angeles *Times*),
and he refused to be called Chandler.

When they first met, Seema did not realize that Chan was the oldest
son of Edward Weston, who was already a well-known photographer.
Chan was skittish about being known as his father's son; unlike his
brothers Brett and Cole, he did not make a career of photography, but
he was close to his father and brothers, just as Seema, her sisters, and
Reva were close—they saw each other often and, like many families,
said little or nothing about their emotional lives.

At the time that Seema and Chan got together, Charis Wilson had
come down from Carmel to live with Edward and his three younger
sons in Santa Monica Canyon. Charis was nineteen when she met
Edward, and he was forty-eight. At first Seema regarded Charis skepti-
cally, wondering whether it was Edward's reputation that attracted this
very young woman to him. As she got to know her better, Seema came
to regard Charis as a goodhearted woman who was deeply in love with
Edward and struggling with the challenge of living in the macho
Weston household.

Whenever Seema and Chan visited Edward and Charis, Edward
would set up an easel and show Seema his newest work. Looking at his
prints, she realized for the first time that photography could be a fine art;
before then she had thought of photographs, including her own, as
snapshots improved upon by the craft she had learned through her years
of working in photo labs. But Edward's photographs moved her as she
was moved by great painting and sculpture.

His work was clean and simple and the lines were finely drawn. I was
overawed with how lovely it was. I thought, this is something new.

Seema had not known artists so dedicated and talented as Edward Weston. His devotion to his work opened a vision for her that was similar to her initial vision of communism. It was something new, something that stirred her, another way of making a better world.

In 1937 Edward received a Guggenheim grant and he and Charis decided to spend a year on the road photographing and writing. The younger boys were living with their mother, so the couple gave up the house they had been renting and filled their car with camping gear and cameras. From time to time they came into Los Angeles and stayed at Chan's house in order to use the darkroom to develop the prints Edward had taken on the road. During those times Seema and Chan stayed with friends or went to a motel, an arrangement Seema and Charis found very odd, but it made perfect sense to Edward and Chan. Of course Edward would have to stay near a darkroom—the most convenient was Chan's.

Seema was shocked and fascinated by the bohemian world of the Westons.

Occasionally all the boys would get together and we'd have an "orgy." They would buy a small barrel of beer, and we'd go to somebody's apartment in Hollywood. There were the four boys and this one time that I remember there were only three girls, myself and two other women. There was a swimming pool there, and they decided to dance near the pool. None of the boys had shirts on—they all wore just their pants and they oiled their upper bodies with a lot of sun oil, so they were quite slippery. We were all having a good time dancing—but I only danced with Chan. The boys might have been going off and having sex with the other girls—I don't know.

Edward Weston loved women and so did his sons. That meant loving as many women as possible. One might give one's heart to one woman, but affection and sex were to be shared with many, a belief that was to become a source of tension between Chan and Seema.

Chan would go out to buy a newspaper, and I never knew who he'd been with by the time he returned. Well, that's an exaggeration, but it gives you a sense of what it was like.

There was no pattern in Chan's family for monogamy or any other conventional behavior. His mother, Flora Chandler Weston, still lived in the house where Chan and his brothers had grown up, only a few blocks away from Chan's place. Flora was a schoolteacher who had grown to dislike her mostly Hispanic students, calling them "dumb." This was a sore point with both Seema and Chan, but it was impossible to argue with Flora.

She had a birthday and a friend was going to take her for a ride, so we said, "After you come back, let's have dinner together." She said, "Fine." . . . [The drive] was windy, so she took off her underwear and put it on her head. We had arranged to have other people there, so the house was full of people, and she walks in with a pair of bloomers on her head. Never took them off.

I think she was trying to prove she was alive. After all, she had raised those four boys whom Edward adored. When Chan was thirteen, his father took him off to Mexico along with Tina Modotti, who was Edward's new mistress. Flora stood on the dock waving goodbye. She yelled to Chan, "Be sure to let me know everything that happens!"

Just before Christmas one year, Flora asked Seema to go shopping with her. Seema watched as Flora bought twenty-three baskets of dried fruit. "They're for my sons' girlfriends," Flora said.

Some of the baskets must have been for Chan's other girlfriends, past and present, for all I knew.

Seema, with help from her family, had cleaned up Chan's house but his tendency to spread things about persisted. She was willing to overlook his sloppiness because of the strong feeling between them, but his resolute non-monogamy was another matter.

I was with Chan close to four years at that period, and the only fly in the ointment was that Chan believed that monogamy was not the natural state for men or women, and so he had many relationships going. I was looking for a good solid relationship that would last, where we had a chance to develop companionship.

He said that he was doing a natural thing, but he wouldn't if I felt bad, and for maybe one day or two days it would last, and back he would go to the same thing. I tried to believe him when he said that it was not going to happen again. I was fooling myself, I knew I was, but it was an addiction and I didn't want to break the addiction.

It was like a magnetic attraction. I never had anything like that before or since, a very strong sexual attraction. It was a continuous process. Very deep, passionate, strong, and needful.

Seema heard that her African-American lover had died in Spain. She didn't want me to use his name. I argued with her—he had died over sixty years ago, a young man with no children. Besides, his name, taken from a Greek myth, was beautiful. She insisted—someone in his family might still be alive and she did not want them to be hurt.

Seema didn't feel free to get in touch with her dead friend's family, because they hadn't known about her affair with him. There would be no memorial service, unless it was a private family gathering. No one advertised their connection with the Abraham Lincoln Battalion in that prewar period, as the whole operation was illegal.

The twenty-eight hundred progressive warriors of the Lincoln Battalion, including many Jews, African Americans, and Hispanic Americans, were looked on with great suspicion in the United States—the FBI called them "premature anti-fascists." The Red Scare was still a potent force, and Seema had learned early to lie low.

One didn't talk about who was in Spain and who wasn't. His friend called me—he had gotten word. He was devastated.

Life with Chan continued to be bumpy. Seema was working, as usual, in a photo lab. At night she and Chan went to meetings to help organize the screenings of films from Spain. Their weekends were a blur of screenings and family events with her family or Chan's, with young Ted often present. She was intensely busy and she liked it that way. If only Chan would stop his constant womanizing. She never knew when he would disappear, only to return to her without apology or explanation.

Thinking of these things one night at home, she reached down absentmindedly and scratched her leg.

"Don't do that, Seema," Chan said, "You'll spread the rash that's on your hands!"

The infection in the open, running, painful sores on her hands and arms had already spread to her legs. She had Metol poisoning, from the developing chemical she had been using. The best dermatologist in Los

Angeles looked at her rash briefly and said, "It's poison oak." Ignoring her protests that she spent most of her time in a photo lab, where there was no poison oak, he handed her a prescription for a useless cream.

She wrote to the manufacturer of Metol, Eastman Kodak, who replied that the only known treatment was a course of arsenic shots, which she wasn't willing to risk. She went on working with Metol, using surgical gloves to protect her hands, struggling with the unaccustomed awkwardness of the gloves, and still the sores persisted.

Charis Weston, who was considered an eccentric because of her interest in alternative healing, suggested that Seema consult a natural healer, Dr. Lovell, who recommended fasting, followed by juices and a cleansing diet. This regimen cleared Seema's sores within a week.

"Chan, please slow down, you're driving much too fast!" Seema gripped the edge of her seat as Chan tore around the curves of the coastal road.

"Oh, this is so exciting!" Leslie leaned over from the back seat and squealed in Chan's ear. Seema stared at her in silence.

When they stopped at a gas station the two women went to the bathroom, and Seema asked Leslie, "Weren't you scared?"

"I was terrified," Leslie answered, as she applied dark red lipstick. "But I didn't want Chan to know."

Seema, who knew that Chan was having an affair with Leslie, was in the process of deciding that she would not tolerate Chan's insistence on his right to make love with whoever attracted him.

"That is one thing I don't want to share."

"But you are equally free to have affairs."

"I don't want to do that, Chan."

She had pretended to have an affair with a friend, even asking him to spend the night once, hoping to make Chan jealous, but it had been useless. Chan had spent the night in his car, and he never said anything to her about it. He was honest in his belief in open relationships, and nothing would change him. Seema was equally convinced of her position.

When Chan started seeing Leslie regularly, Seema decided she would leave him. She went to stay with Tama while she decided what to do next.

figure 21. Seema, Virginia and Ansel Adams, Best's Studio,
Yosemite, ca. 1940. Courtesy of Ann Adams Helms.

3

1938—41: yosemite

ansel

EDWARD WESTON INVITED SEEMA FOR LUNCH.

"Ansel Adams is looking for a darkroom assistant out at Yosemite. Are you interested?"

Seema was grateful for the chance to leave Los Angeles. And the opportunity to work for Ansel Adams, a rising photographer! She hadn't seen his work yet, but she had heard wonderful things about him.

"Yes," Seema said. "Yes, I am interested."

Seema met the Adamses at a restaurant in San Francisco. They looked their role as upper-crust San Franciscans, Ansel wearing a business suit, and Virginia in a stylish dress with a hat and gloves. In the Valley, Seema would learn, they dressed much more informally. She found them consistently kind, well-bred, and unassuming.

Virginia managed the studio shop in Yosemite, left to her by her father, Harry Best, a landscape painter who spent each summer with his family in the Valley. In 1906 he was given a concession by the government to sell his paintings and other artwork in the park.

Virginia was raised in Yosemite, and Ansel, an aspiring concert pianist who worked at summer jobs there and took photographs as a hobby, met her at her family home when they were both in their late teens. They were engaged to marry in 1923; Ansel broke off the engagement, only to return after several years. Virginia waited for him patiently while he gradually

figure 22. Ansel Adams, Yosemite, photo by Seema
Weatherwax, ca. 1939. Courtesy of Seema Weatherwax.

made his choice of photography over music, a decision that meant he could work in the wilderness he loved. They married in 1928, and their son Michael was born in 1933, followed by their daughter Anne in 1935.

In 1936, after Virginia's father died, the Adamses moved to Yosemite full-time. Best's Studio, with its sales of artifacts, cards, and prints of Ansel's photographs, became the main support of the family, as Ansel struggled to build his career. Crowds of people came to the Valley each summer; there were already complaints about noise and pollution from cars and campfires. The visitors were a threat to the Adamses' beloved wilderness, but their business was essential to the studio.

At first Imogen Cunningham's son Ron Partridge, Ansel's assistant, helped with the work, but as business expanded the Adamses realized that they needed to hire an experienced photofinisher. The job would include developing film, making contact prints and enlargements for customers, and making prints as needed of Ansel's photographs.

Once the Adamses saw Seema's portfolio and talked with her about the work that was needed, she was hired. It was unusual at that time for a woman to be hired for that range of darkroom work, but her gender was never mentioned, a welcome change after all the discrimination and harassment Seema had encountered in her commercial jobs.

She returned to Los Angeles to quit her job, pack her things, and say goodbye to friends and family. When she told Chan about her new job he asked if he could come and visit her.

"We'll see," she replied.

Several weeks later she took the train back to San Francisco, where Ansel met her, and they drove together to Yosemite.

yosemite

It was early spring, the snow was melting, and there had been a big flood just before. The Merced River was raging, the road from Merced to the Valley was only one lane, and on one side were precipices. On the other side was a raging river, practically on the edge of the one lane. I wondered what I was doing there! It was exciting! I was scared, but I wasn't scared enough to say, Let's go back.

"Tell me about yourself," Ansel said to Seema. "How did you get interested in photography?"

The hours passed quickly as they talked, and soon they arrived at the Valley Viewpoint, where Seema saw the Yosemite Valley floor for the first time.

Everything was beautiful, lush green—it was spring, the waterfalls were rushing all over in this basin full of colossal cliffs. I never got over that. Every time I saw it, it was thrilling.

figure 23. Feet Firmly Planted, Yosemite, photo by Seema Weatherwax, ca. 1939. Courtesy of Seema Weatherwax.

They drove straight to Government Center, which consisted of a ranger station, a post office, a small grocery, and Best's Studio. Virginia welcomed Seema and showed her around. The Adamses' simple living quarters, light and spacious, were attached to the studio by a stairway at the back. The darkroom was a separate building behind the studio, with two cabins a bit further along. Seema was given the larger cabin.

It had a large living room, then there was a bedroom, and a back porch all enclosed that also had a bed, and a regular kitchen and bathroom, well heated with an oil stove and an electric stove and lighting and everything very modern, very nice. The front porch was open, and I used to sit there and sometimes do spotting on pictures that had to be touched up. Sometimes I just sat and listened to the music of the falls.

As soon as she had settled in, Seema went to see what work she would be doing. Ansel showed her around the darkroom, the nicest she had ever seen, gleaming with stainless steel counters and spotless equipment. There was work waiting, and he said, "Make yourself at home."

A short while later she came out. Ansel was looking over some prints.

"It's all very well," she said, "but how am I to wash prints when I can't reach the faucets?"

Ansel burst out laughing. He was over six feet, and Ron Partridge, his previous assistant, was a tall young man. At barely five foot one, Seema could only reach the water faucets by jumping up, and she couldn't turn them. Some adjustments had to be made to the plumbing before she could work in the darkroom.

A few days later, Seema sat in a rocking chair on the front porch of her cabin, looking at the afternoon light as it filtered down through the trees. It was so peaceful; she could hear the rush of water from Yosemite Falls, just up the path. The tension of the past few months began to subside.

Virginia Adams came up the path from the studio. She seemed surprised to see Seema sitting out on the porch, and she smiled hesitantly.

"I hope you're going to be able to meet the deadline, Seema."

"What do you mean?"

"Well, we promised people their work would be ready this afternoon."

"But it's all done!"

"Really?" Virginia could hardly believe it. How could Seema have finished all that work so soon?

Virginia was the angel of the Adams household, taking full responsibility for raising their two children, running the house, entertaining their many guests, and managing the studio. Seema looked up to her.

She was unobtrusive, yet firm. Once she realized I could do the work, she relaxed, and we became friends. There was no question of the need to have the work done. That was easy for me because I knew that type of work very well. But I had to think in terms of how Ansel wanted it.

You can print from the same negative in a million different ways, by changing the paper, the contrast of the paper, how dark and light it should be. Each person sees it a little differently. I was able to duplicate what I saw Ansel saw in the pictures that he took. That's why I have a few pictures from his negatives that I've forgotten whether he printed them or I printed them, and I don't think anyone else would recognize the difference. I could see things pretty close to what he was seeing.

I asked if she ever compared Ansel's work with Edward Weston's.

I felt there was more power in Ansel's work than in Edward's. There was less of this feeling of serenity and beauty for the sake of beauty. There seemed to be more emotion.

Because of his nature, his work was more powerful. I don't know if everybody gets the same feeling and I don't know whether it's because I was working closely with him and learning at the same time why he was doing it that way. He would say, "Now I think to bring out that just a little bit more, it needs just a bit . . ." and I would begin to learn.

Edward Weston, who was meticulous in the darkroom, prided himself on creating his photographs as he took them; he printed exactly what he had photographed. Ansel Adams placed as much emphasis on his darkroom work as on his composition of the original photograph. Working with him, Seema got a new appreciation of the whole process of photography, from the placement of the camera through the selection of filters and lenses to the final developing of the print. She often went out on shoots with Ansel, and she learned how he looked at a landscape, how he judged light and framed his pictures. It was all easy for her, as natural as the way she judged the density of a negative in the darkroom, and all the while she and Ansel would joke and laugh.

As she became part of the Adams family circle, always welcome at their dinner table, she heard many discussions of the art and craft of photography by the most influential practitioners of the time. Edward Weston, Ansel Adams, and Imogen Cunningham agreed that photography was a valid art form. Imogen was an inspiration to Seema, a feisty older woman who was focused on her own work and who spoke her mind freely. Dorothea Lange, a close friend of the Adamses, argued with Ansel and Edward that photography was best used as a documentary form with social and political import, referring to her own powerful photographs of people caught in the Dust Bowl and the Depression. Ansel responded with his deep-seated belief in the importance of nature, interpreted by the thoughtful photographer.

Edward insisted on the pristine quality of the images he "discovered" with his camera. Imogen felt patronized by his admiration of some, but by no means all, of her images. Her happy use of accidental double exposures and damaged negatives challenged the "pure image" ideas of Edward and Ansel.

Seema accepted Edward and Ansel's orthodox ideas about photographic art, and she admired Imogen and Dorothea for their rapport with ordinary people and their willingness to challenge convention. Edward was able to display his female nudes as part of a recognized art tradition, but Imogen's first exhibit of male nudes in 1915 had created such a scandal that she put them away for the next fifty years.

Seema said Imogen broke the ice for others by exhibiting her photographs of her husband, Roi Partridge, posing nude in the woods above Berkeley.

She had three children and a husband at home, and she used what she had. What she had was a naked husband, so she photographed him.

Seema seemed surprised when I burst out laughing, then she chuckled, acknowledging that her old friend had been a real pioneer.

These arguments about form and content in photography were new and exciting in the years when they were all struggling for recognition and having to earn a living in the midst of inventing their work. Compared to their immediate concerns, the escalating war in Europe seemed remote, but the reports of war added urgency to Ansel's insistence that nature and the artist's vision of nature could be healing forces in a difficult world.

For Seema, the different perspectives joining art, politics, and nature brought together familiar strands from her childhood. She felt at home with these discussions without feeling a need to take a position of her own. Like her family's dedication to communism, the art she knew in Yosemite offered a vision of a better world. Her sense of herself in that world was as a supporter, not a prime mover or creator.

Nonetheless, she bought herself a camera and began to take her own photographs.

I had a chance to buy a very good camera, that was my super-Ikonta B, almost as soon as I came, because they could get it at cost price, which was better than wholesale. I was inspired by the scenery to try to do something for myself, so wherever I went, with Ansel or any of the others who came there to photograph, I would take my camera with me and photograph what I liked.

I did make contact prints from all my negatives, and I made a few enlargements, not too many. I never showed Ansel or the others the stuff that I printed for myself.

That first summer in Yosemite, Chan came to visit.

Seema showed me a postcard, sent by Edward Weston to his oldest son, which she was given after Chan died. It was a plain postal card, written in a large, legible scrawl: "arrived S.F. last night from Yosemite. Cole, Neil, Sam, here. You had better write your sweet, lonely little girl, Sophie, unless you want to lose her! We return to Carmel tomorrow. Love, Dad"

Very soon after I got there Chan started to phone and ask if he could come out to see me. He wrote me letters and said he missed me. And he sent wires that said, "Could I come out next weekend?" By this time, everybody in the Valley knew that I had a boyfriend called Chan. The postman used to say, "Are you going to answer this postcard? What are you going to tell him?" The Western Union man would come over and he'd say, "Shall I wait for a reply? Are you going to say yes or no? Should he come next weekend?"

seeing more

Seema leaned back in her chair sipping her favorite cocktail, a mint julep. They had gathered around a small campfire in back of the studio for drinks before dinner. Virginia was fond of such small rituals, very much appreciated by her guests, and she moved quietly back and forth, helping the cook in the kitchen, making sure the table was set as she liked it, seeing that glasses were filled and refilled.

Chan was visiting for the weekend, as he did often that first summer Seema spent in Yosemite, making the long drive every two or three weeks. He sometimes brought eight-year-old Ted, but more often he came alone, seeing Ted on the weekends he was in Los Angeles. Seema wondered who else was with him on those weekends.

The current she felt connecting her to Chan was as strong as ever.

The Adamses welcomed Chan as Edward's son, Seema's partner, and as himself; he fit in easily with all the talk of photography, art, the environment, and politics. Ansel was passionately interested in these subjects, and his vitality and gentle joking drew people to him. There were many guests, up to ten or twelve people around the dinner table, and they would sit a long while over dinner, dessert, and coffee; afterward they would adjourn to the studio, where there was a grand piano and plenty of room for people to sit around. Ansel, who was a gifted pianist, occasionally played, and Virginia was sometimes prevailed on to sing. She had a fine voice and Ansel had encouraged her to become a concert singer, but she was more interested in raising a family and supporting his work. They invited others to join in the entertainment, which often turned hilarious.

Seema felt entirely at home in this atmosphere, which reminded her of her childhood and the many gatherings hosted by her parents. When Chan was present she was content to sit back with his arm around her and enjoy the entertainment. On her own, she was more apt to dance with Edward or one of the other men, and she found it easy to join the flow of joking and banter.

On weekend days when there was no pressing work for the studio, Seema and Chan went hiking in the Valley, and she felt the extraordinary beauty of the place like a healing salve. She realized how stressful

figure 24. Seema with Graflex, Yosemite,
ca. 1940. Courtesy of Seema Weatherwax.

figure 25. Ansel Adams with view camera, photo by Seema
Weatherwax, ca. 1940. Courtesy of Seema Weatherwax.

her life in Los Angeles had been, how peaceful she felt in Yosemite. Chan took a photograph of her as she sat on a great boulder in the middle of a mountain stream, leaning back on one arm, her dark hair falling back to her shoulders. She looked up toward the trees, her face relaxed and calm. The same Valley energy that had brought Ansel back to health when he first came to Yosemite as a sickly adolescent was now working its magic on Seema.

When Seema met Ansel, he had already started to build the career that was his way of expressing the fire inside him. His father had always encouraged his creativity, first in music; young Ansel thought he would be a concert pianist. Photography was less intentional; his first memorable picture, taken when he was fourteen, with the Kodak box camera his parents gave him on their first family trip to Yosemite, was accidental—he tripped the shutter while falling backward from a boulder. As he grew up, finding ways to spend all his summers at Yosemite, photography became more and more important to him, and the response to his photographs helped him to decide on this as a career.

By the time Seema met him, the fire inside Ansel was a steady, warming blaze. Energetic and curious herself, she found that she could keep pace with his boundless vitality. After a long stretch, ten or twelve hours in the darkroom finishing some pressing work, they would relax by drinking and partying into the night, then go back to work early the next morning.

She never could identify her own perfectionist streak with Ansel's artistry. For her, photography was a trade, something to be done quickly and well, with a minimum of fuss. She considered herself a technician, not an artist, but the artist in her recognized Ansel and reached out to him.

When I used to work in different labs I wasn't thinking emotionally about the pictures. I was just making good technical prints, but in Yosemite I began to think more about what else was there in the print, and how to portray what one saw.

When I looked at those trees that you see in that photograph, I wanted to bring out the different textures with the light shining on them. I thought, Oh, that's beautiful—it isn't just one glob of trees—every tree is a little bit different, and it has these claws underneath, which are the roots, so it was very dramatic to me (fig. 25).

I became more analytical about why I was doing or seeing things, and that I learned from watching Ansel respond. It was the first time I'd had leisure to do anything except work from nine to five in the darkroom, so I began to feel more creative.

By the time I got to Ansel I was open to trying to think, I want to see more in the shadows, or I want to see more in the clouds or . . . I realized that you had to understand what you were doing the whole way through.

ANOTHER TRY

She took her suitcase from the car, thanking the friend who had driven her from Yosemite. A buzz of voices came from the little house and as soon as she walked in Chan came over with a glass in his hand.

"Seema! I'm so glad you're here! Sorry about the crowd, but this party was arranged before I knew you were coming and I couldn't really change it."

"Of course not, Chan," she said, as he took her case and gave her the drink. She was ready to recommit to a relationship with Chan—he had shown her that he really cared for her, driving the long way to Yosemite so many times during the summer. She had arranged with Ansel and Virginia that she would go down to Los Angeles for a couple of months now that things were slowing down in the Valley. They would mail some of the photofinishing to her, and she could use Chan's darkroom.

She knew many of the guests and was chatting with several when a woman she didn't know came over.

"I hope you don't spoil my relationship with Chan—it's going so well," she purred. Seema was speechless.

Her realization that nothing had changed was still strong as she told me about it so many years later.

What could I say to her? I came there to be with Chan. He'd asked me to come there. I couldn't say, "Stop fooling yourself. Why the hell do you think I'm here?"

figure 26. Chan Weston, by Dorothea Lange,
ca. 1938. Courtesy of Jason Weston.

*She and the rest of them left me there with him. I couldn't walk out just
like that and say, "To hell with you." I still was not ready to do that. I
thought perhaps he'd been playing around while I wasn't there. I wasn't
thinking rationally, because I was so involved with him. I wanted the
relationship to continue that badly.*

After a few weeks Seema cut short her time in Los Angeles and
returned to Yosemite.

*"Don't write to me, don't phone me, and don't come. I will not
answer anything that comes from you and I will not have you visit me.
This is the end."*

I heard steel in her voice as she repeated this to me.

*This time, he knew I really meant it. Before when I said I was going to
leave him, I wasn't ready. But now, I felt, I can't stand any more of this*

business, not knowing where I was, what I was, what was going to happen the next day. I felt like a weight was lifted from my shoulders.

tHe vaLLey

She went back to Yosemite, to the friends who meant so much to her, but now she was without a partner. Those were challenging years, when she was in and out of love, living in the midst of great natural beauty and an outpouring of art, with the great variations of the seasons mirroring her emotional ups and downs.

When she first went to Yosemite, she thought she would learn to ski, but when she saw how frequently the skiers broke their bones, she realized she could not afford the risk. She needed to be able to work if she was to stay there, so she gave up the idea of skiing and learned to skate instead.

My niece Joy was there. Yosemite was such a fairyland in winter—I was just enchanted with everything. We went together to buy skates, and Joy strapped hers on her little feet, then she skated off as if she had been skating all her life. I could have wrung her neck, the little brat! I could feel my ankles buckling beneath me, and I was so afraid—I made a joke of it and everyone laughed. To this day Joy remembers how she could skate, and how mad I pretended to be, but no one knew I was so very scared. I did things even though I was afraid, in those days.

There was a tension between Seema's identification with the Adamses and their friends and her position as a paid employee who could not afford to be laid up, even for a few weeks. She was not timid physically but she had a terrible fear of poverty, of not being able to earn her way, that went back to her cross-country trip in the twenties, and much further back, to memories of a bowl of slop in a prison cell.

Unemployment, already high in 1928 when Seema set out from New Jersey with Jim, her first husband, was much more severe in the late 1930s when she was working in Yosemite. It was not until the United States entered the war that full employment was restored, and not until after the war that the economy would be fully recovered from the series of events called the Great Depression. Those who suffered from it bore the scars long afterward.

figure 27. Joy Sands and Ted Weston, Yosemite, photo by
Seema Weatherwax, ca. 1938. Courtesy of Seema Weatherwax.

Seema's sense of her need to earn a secure living prevented her from feeling free to follow photography as something more than an occasional indulgence.

"Do you think you could have been a good photographer?" I asked, thinking that she certainly had high standards of comparison.

Yes, if it hadn't been for my own sexism. I thought I had to support a man to do his work. I didn't have the guts that Imogen and Dorothea had—I always thought I had to earn my living by getting a regular job. It never occurred to me that I could go out on my own and get the support I needed to become a photographer.

I took a lot of very good photographs, but I never showed them to Ansel, because I felt that his work was so important. I never showed them to Edward. Chan was the only one of the photographers who ever saw my work, and he thought I should do more. He was a photographer on the same level as I was.

She was fiercely loyal to the Adamses and to the face they presented to the world, a devoted couple, dedicated to their family as well as to Ansel's work. However, she saw that Ansel, charismatic in social gatherings, had difficulty relating to his own children.

He didn't know how to put his arms around his daughter and tell her he loved her. He was very warm and hospitable, but he didn't know how to express affection to his children.

"Ansel, I'm leaving now for the weekend. I've given the telephone number at my sister Tama's in case you need to call."

Ansel was bent over his work, but as she walked out he called out to her gruffly. "I hope you're coming back!"

She smiled to herself. When she returned to Yosemite after her final breakup with Chan, Ansel simply put his arm around her and held her tight. He was a big man, with long arms and legs. He had broken his nose in a childhood fall, and its crookedness gave an elfish twist to his face, with his bright eyes and wide grin. He was gentle, but ruthless about his art, and as his ruthlessness was entirely impersonal, it made him few enemies.

Seema was ruthless when she went single-mindedly in pursuit of something she cared about, whether it was setting up a studio in Tahiti, insisting on a relationship that met her standards, or instructing Jason Weston, Chan's grandson, to print her old negatives the way she thought they should be printed. Ansel was a worthy ally for her, presenting stiff challenges with imperturbable good humor.

Ansel liked to be a devil's advocate—so one night when there was a bunch of us at dinner, mostly conservatives, he just asked casually if anybody there knew "The Internationale." Of course nobody else did, and he said, "Do you happen to know it, Seema?" I said, "Yes," because if anybody confronts me face on I do not lie about it, so I said, "Yes I do, but I can't sing. But if everybody will join with me and get into the tune, I'll sing it."

So we sat, about ten of us around the table, bankers, financial people, and we all sang "The Internationale." I sang the words and they kind of hummed along and joined in. It was fun. I also felt like kicking Ansel in the ass for proposing it, because it could have been different; but they had accepted me to the point that I was friends with most of these people already, and they took it in good spirit. He shouldn't oughta have done it, but he did!

> Arise, ye prisoners of starvation!
> Arise, ye wretched of the earth!
> For justice thunders condemnation,
> A better world's in birth.
> No more, tradition's chains shall bind us,
> Arise ye slaves, no more in thrall.
> The earth shall rise on new foundations,
> We have been naught, we shall be all.
>
> 'Tis the final conflict,
> Let us stand in our place.
> The international working class
> Shall be the human race!

She sang quietly, in a high thin voice, forgetting my presence, as if she were among her old friends, years and years ago, singing for all her bright beliefs.

Conservative Americans were wary of "Reds," their suspicions fueled by anti-Soviet propaganda and the stories about Stalin that had already begun to circulate. To many Americans, the Fascists and the Communists were simply two sides of a general European threat to good Yankee sense. Ansel was a Roosevelt supporter, liberal in his politics, not one to embrace an ideology other than his own ideas about photography, fine art, and the environment.

He was often away from Yosemite, but there was always plenty of work for Seema. When Dorothea Lange, shooting photographs for the Farm Security Administration in the American South, had no darkroom where she could develop her negatives, she sent them to Yosemite, where Seema and her young assistant, Ray Wolfe, developed them. Ray was seventeen, a bright young man studying biochemistry, very capable but unfamiliar with the holders Seema used for Dorothea's 4 × 5 negatives. One day when he was alone in the darkroom he didn't fasten the negatives properly and some of them slipped down. Ray called Seema, who came running. Although they managed to retrieve some of the negatives, others were scratched or overdeveloped. Dorothea was understanding, but Seema was remorseful about the accident.

Outside of work there was always something wonderful to do. She bought an old bicycle and rode it around the Valley. There were several thousand people living in Yosemite year round, and she made friends among the rangers and other park employees. She collected memories of all the seasons: the summer Firefall, when park staff would push burning logs over the top of Glacier Point to fall thousands of feet in a cascade of bright embers; winter nights when new-fallen snow lay fresh on the meadows. Late one winter night she was walking home alone after visiting friends and she saw two coyotes racing along in the snow, chasing deer. Although she knew the coyotes were preoccupied with the deer, she was terrified until she got back to her cabin.

Best of all, for Seema, were the parties.

We had birthday celebrations—the senior Adamses would come up for the children's birthdays—and we'd have a lot of parties. Once a week they had dancing at the Ahwahnee Hotel, and occasionally I went there with one of the young assistants. They had New Year's Eve parties and the Bracebridge dinner, which Ansel directed during the time I was there. That was a fantastic affair. The sculptor Benny Bufano was my escort to one of the Bracebridge dinners; another time Richard Dyer Bennett, who was a wonderful madrigal singer, came to my table and played his lute for me.

When Ansel and Edward Weston gave the first Camera Forum at Yosemite in 1940, Seema assisted, going along on shoots and helping in the darkroom with the basics of developing and printing film.

He got all the visiting teachers together and said, "I want every one of you to stand on exactly the same spot and photograph that object over there." And they did. Then he said, "Now, I want every one of you to go back to the darkroom and print your own stuff." And it was very very different. He said, "One of you saw the clouds, and printed for the clouds; another one saw the shadows and printed for dramatic effect," and so on. He pointed out how different they were, because every one saw and wanted to bring out something different. And that's where the emotional thing, what you see, comes in. So this was a lesson for me, because I knew it as a fact, but I'd never seen it illustrated so clearly as when he did that.

People came from New York, from southern California, and from the Midwest. It wasn't easy to stay in Yosemite unless you camped out or unless you had a lot of money, so the people who came were wealthy. They had to come with a good camera and have a little knowledge of photography, because this was an intermediate workshop, to show how Ansel took pictures.

Ansel and Edward teased Seema constantly, about how she wore a fur coat when they were shooting high on the trails because she was always cold, about her height, about anything that would get a good-humored response.

We'd all get together in the evening and talk. Ansel would play the piano, and Edward and I helped make the party livelier.

One evening when they were all sitting together in the studio, Seema turned to Edward and whispered something to him. They got up and left. When they returned, Seema was wearing a tight-fitting short leotard with a fringed scarf wrapped around her waist and covering her hips, a string of beads, and high heels; Edward sported a French beret and bathing trunks. They performed a wild Parisian apache dance in which Seema flung her beads over Edward's head, then he threw her down and straddled her, while Ansel accompanied them at the piano, his head thrown back in laughter as the guests cheered and clapped (figs. 28a, b, c).

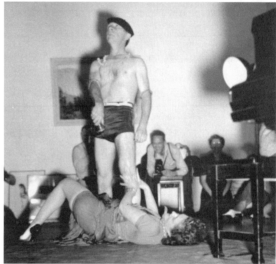

figures 28a, b, c.
Seema and
Edward Weston,
apache dance,
Yosemite, 1940.
Courtesy of Seema
Weatherwax.

Seema's family came often to visit her in Yosemite. The first time Freda and Frank came they were prepared to camp out, having no idea that Seema was living in comfort in a well-equipped cabin. She chuckled, having deliberately let them believe she was living a rugged life, and the story became a family joke.

Tama came with Joy, who grew up with happy memories of Yosemite in every season; sometimes Aurel, Tama's second husband, accompanied them. Tama had met Aurel Leitner in 1936, after she returned from New York; they fell in love and soon married. Aurel was born and raised in Hungary, where he had studied art and music; he came to New York as a promising young concert pianist. At age twenty-five, he lost his left arm in a car accident that ended his concert career. He became a successful graphic artist, working for the WPA during the New Deal, but he remained shy and withdrawn about his handicap. Tama told me she once bought him sheet music for playing piano with one hand, and he put it away and never mentioned it. But in Yosemite, Ansel's warmth drew Aurel out to the point where, to Tama's astonishment and delight, he and Ansel once played a duet on the grand piano in the studio.

Reva came to the Valley, sometimes alone, sometimes with Sam. She loved walking on the trails. Ansel welcomed her, calling her "Mamele," little mother, and praising her for teaching Seema to make *floymentsimmes*, brisket of beef stewed with prunes, a favorite at the Adamses' dinner table.

"Everyone used to count the pits on their plate to see how much they had eaten," Seema said, as she served me a large, fragrant helping of the famous dish.

Seema's recipe for floymentsimmes
First, you get a brisket of beef, if you can find it, if not, a good chuck or roast, not too lean, about one to two pounds, and cut it in chunks.

Then you sauté onions and add the beef and a little liquid, and put it in the oven, like a pot roast, at 350°, covered, until it is almost tender.

Meanwhile, wash half a pound of prunes and add these to the beef when it is almost tender. Peel some yams and cut them in chunks, enough for maybe half a large yam for each person. Add the yams once the meat is tender. Add water to barely cover the yams, and a little sugar and lemon juice. Keep basting and turning until all is tender and well-blended, maybe another half hour after you've added the yams. Add a little salt, and serve.

fine art

During the slow winter season Seema often accompanied Ansel to San Francisco, where she assisted him in the large darkroom he had made in the basement of his parents' house on Lake Street at 24th Avenue, overlooking the Presidio with its trees and green spaces.

On one of these trips she stood on the board put in for her benefit around the edge of the huge developing tank, watching as the image of Half Dome in the snow emerged on the large floating sheet of photographic paper. At the instant that it looked right to her, she pulled the paper out of the developer and immersed it in another tank of solution. When she had completed the processing Ansel came over to have a look.

"It's almost there," he said, "But I think just a tiny bit darker would bring out the cliffs better, and the shadows."

He cut another sheet of paper from a huge roll and printed the same negative again, using the oversized enlarger. He placed the new print in the developing tank, waiting until it was exactly as he wanted it, then he pulled it out and finished the process.

I could see that the tiny difference in timing brought out texture in the shadows and in the highlights. Ansel never criticized my work. Only once in a while he would say, "I think that needs just a second longer in the developer." And I would realize he was right.

Ansel gave her the first print, the one that was not quite dark enough.

He never signed that mural. He wouldn't sign anything that he didn't print. He said the printing part is just as important as taking the negative. You can make a beautiful negative, and you can make a very bad print. You've got to be on top of every phase of it. You've got to develop the negative and print and develop the print, and bring it to what you want it to be, otherwise you should not sign it, because it's not your work completely.

In San Francisco as in the Valley, Seema and Ansel worked long hours; then they took time to play, with equal intensity.

I met a group of people who were alien to anything that I'd met before, especially to my way of thinking, which remained very radical through all these years. I had friends in the Junior League, which sounds really far-fetched, but as individuals they were nice.

Communist-minded Seema found herself hobnobbing with the wealthiest families in San Francisco and enjoying herself hugely. When I asked her how she reconciled her political beliefs with her Junior League friendships, she repeated what she had said about her first encounter with Marxism in the twenties.

The system was what was wrong, not the people. They were good people, and I liked being with them.

She spent some of her salary to buy a couple of elegant black evening dresses, and she had her hair done weekly at the Valley beauty parlor.

"I was trying to make it lie down," she explained to me, with an embarrassed laugh. "That's why it looks different in the photographs of me in that period."

Ansel took Seema to concerts at Stern's, a private outdoor amphitheater where famous musicians performed for select audiences. They drove across the Bay to visit Imogen Cunningham at her small, cluttered house in Oakland. Imogen, who loved to cook, made big pots of stew for them, and she had jam simmering on the kitchen stove as they sat around the table talking and joking.

I thought she was a very good camera person. I enjoyed her opinions about the political scene, the social scene, the photographic scene. She was very much for the people. She was always poor when I knew her—I don't mean dirt poor, but she never had real money. Her way of living was very modest.

She was feisty, very open, and she was knowledgeable about what was going on in the world. She had very decided, mostly progressive opinions on many subjects. I beat around the bush a little bit, but she came straight out and said what she thought. She was quite a lot older than me, but you know, this age thing is something that I don't care about. Neither did she, apparently.

Once, when Seema and Ansel drove down to visit Edward and Charis Weston in the Carmel highlands, it was foggy on the coast road, but the fog lifted as they approached the hill above Wildcat Creek, where Neil Weston had built a large cabin for his father and Charis on her father's land. Charis came out from her small writing studio at the back to greet them and soon Edward emerged from his darkroom, shouting, "Come and see my new prints," so they crowded in to peer at the prints as he took them down from the drying rack and set them up, one at a time, on an easel.

That night after dinner they all helped to clear away the dishes and Edward washed up at the small sink in the kitchen corner of the one-room cabin. Charis poured drinks and put a tango record on the Victrola, saying, "Seema, you look like a tango dancer in that beautiful dress."

Edward grabbed Seema, who was wearing a close-fitting black sheath printed with large white flowers, and he began to whirl her around the room. They finished with a fiercely focused step toward Ansel and a decisive stomp of Seema's heel on the wood floor.

In the summer of 1940, when Ansel organized the Pageant of Photography for the Golden Gate Exposition in San Francisco, Seema went up to help with darkroom work and last-minute touchups for the exhibit. When Ansel went off with visitors—one of them was Diego Rivera, who was in San Francisco painting a mural—Seema took Ansel's place at the exhibit, greeting people and answering questions.

It was still new for people to think of photography as a fine art, and Ansel had taken great care to present the exhibit in that light, including a wide range of work, mostly American, ranging from some of the earliest daguerreotypes of the previous century to recent experiments of Man Ray. He showed work from the Farm Security Administration, the New York Photo League, and *Life* magazine; artists working individually: Edward Weston, Berenice Abbott, Eugene Atget, Margaret Bourke-White, Paul Strand, Brett Weston, Cedric Wright; and his own work, demonstrating, as he wrote in the catalog, that "photography is, in fact, a decisive American art."

The French pavilion kept sending over champagne cocktails, which Seema dutifully sipped, although she did not like the drink.

She was beginning to ask herself, "Where is my life going?" She enjoyed her work for Ansel and she knew exactly what she was doing in the darkroom. But although she was close to Ansel and Virginia and she dated some of the men who lived in the Valley, her life was not entirely satisfactory. She missed having a companion. She had a home with the Adamses, but she wanted her own home.

This life in Yosemite was wonderful, but it was leading nowhere. I was open to starting with someone else.

news from outside

Every few months Seema went down to Los Angeles for a long weekend to visit family and friends, all active in the movement as Communists or fellow travelers—"progressives" was the term she used. From them she heard news about the issues of the day: the Spanish Civil War, farm labor, and the struggle against racism. She brought back to the Valley a recording of Billie Holiday singing "Strange Fruit" at Cafe Society in New York and played the song for her book club. Seema spoke to them about racism in terms of her own experiences, feeling pleased when several of them went out and bought the record. "Strange Fruit" had enormous impact on the Popular Front—it was a haunting song about lynching written by Lewis Allan (pseudonym for Abel Meeropol, a Jewish schoolteacher from New York who later adopted and raised as his own the two sons of Ethel and Julius Rosenberg after their parents were executed as Russian spies).

Following the refusal of England, France, and the U.S. to sell arms to the Spanish Loyalists, the Loyalists were defeated by Franco and the fascist forces. The survivors of the Abraham Lincoln Battalion, including some of Seema's friends, returned home from Spain. In the summer of 1939 Stalin signed a nonaggression pact with Hitler. Then in the fall the Soviets and Germany invaded and partitioned Poland.

Many Americans, disillusioned by Stalin's actions, left the Communist Party at that time, but Seema, who never identified the Party with its

figure 29. *When I took this photograph I was with Edward and Ansel.*
They thought it was too foggy, but I decided that in spite of the fog
I was going to take that picture. Fog Below Point Lobos, photo by
Seema Weatherwax, ca. 1940. Courtesy of Seema Weatherwax.

leaders, and who was not involved in any direct political work during the
time she was in Yosemite, accepted the Party argument that the Soviets
were acting for purely defensive reasons. Her cousin Liza, Seema's best
friend from Boston days, had married an engineer and moved with him
to Moscow where she found work as a translator—Seema felt a close connection to the Soviet Union through her correspondence with Liza.

The Party was in the forefront of the struggle against racism in the 1930s and '40s. Racism and poverty were two issues that Seema knew firsthand, and her need to find a movement that would work against these injustices went bone deep in her. She was used to arguments and disagreements about what the Party was doing, and for the most part she ignored them.

She was often in the position of explaining her beliefs to her apolitical Valley friends, as when she refused to cross a picket line to enter their favorite restaurant in Merced. "You can go in if you want," she said, "but I can't. I'll wait in the car for you if you like." Her friends, though puzzled, got back in the car with her and they drove to another restaurant.

Another time, when the friends were shopping in Merced, the others bought silk stockings, but Seema chose rayon.

"Silk is better, why don't you buy it?" Nan asked, stroking the soft smooth fabric with careful fingers.

"I won't buy anything from Japan," Seema answered. At that time American Communists and progressives were boycotting Japanese goods because of Japan's military preparations.

About a week later Nan handed me a couple of pairs of silk stockings and said, "You didn't want to buy them, so I bought them for you."

I was horrified.

I said, "Don't you understand? It wasn't a question of my buying them, it was a question of buying them, period, of supporting them. And you did for me what I wouldn't do for myself—I can't accept them."

And I didn't.

In June 1940, as Seema was helping Ansel prepare his exhibit of photographs for the San Francisco Exposition, Hitler toured occupied Paris and the British recognized Charles de Gaulle as the leader of the Free French. In July, while the exhibit was on, the Soviets invaded Lithuania, Latvia, and Estonia. In the United States most people ignored these distant events. The general American mood was one of isolationism.

On September 7 the Germans began their *Blitzkrieg* and bombs rained down on English cities. The United States passed a bill for military conscription on September 16, 1940. That fall, American Communists and other progressives demonstrated for peace and campaigned for

President Roosevelt as their strongest hope against American fascism. He was re-elected in November. On her visits to Los Angeles, Seema went to demonstrations for peace.

She went in October, near Tama's birthday, when things were slowing down in Yosemite, and again in the spring, before the busy summer season, sharing a bedroom with Joy in the house on Windsor Avenue where Tama and Aurel lived with Reva and Sam. They all loved the house, Spanish-style, covered in stucco, two stories high with a large living room and a bay window that overlooked the Silver Lake reservoir at the bottom of the hill.

figure 30. Jack and Seema Weatherwax, Los Angeles,
ca. 1942. Courtesy of Seema Weatherwax.

4

1940–84: Jack

THIS MAN IN LOS ANGELES

SEEMA MET JACK WEATHERWAX FOR THE FIRST TIME IN OCTOBER 1940, at a party she went to with Tama and Aurel. She was dating several men at that time and she was not immediately impressed by Jack, but when he invited her to join some friends at his mother's house the next evening, she agreed to go. They sat around the fireplace and Jack read from a piece he was working on about the Chinese poet Li Po.

He read about two pages, and it was so poetic and so beautiful, about Li Po and the woman he loved, that I felt this was a man I really wanted to know. So, when he asked if I would go out with him on New Year's Eve, which was the next time I was coming down to Los Angeles, I accepted, and I found that I liked him very much.

"A god in exile," they called him. For he was handsome and tall and very strong. Six and one-half feet he towered, and he could pull the tail out of a living ox. And yet, of all the Six Idlers of the Bamboo Valley, not one could be more gentle, not one could play the sweet lute more melodiously, and not one could write poems like his—poems that could turn a woman's heart to tears within her, or break it with joy, or set it afire for eternity with an unquenchable flame of longing; poems that were like the breathing of a temple bell, calling men to prayer, or like the music of

figure 31. Jack Weatherwax, photo by Seema Weatherwax,
Los Angeles, ca. 1943. Courtesy of Seema Weatherwax.

yellow wine bubbling from a golden cask, inviting them to drink,
or like the roar of a tiger, terrifying and chilling them and driving them to blood and death; poems that one day would shake
the very foundations of the Five Sacred Mountains of the Middle
Flower Kingdom.

—from "The Lady Yang," by John M. Weatherwax
(unpublished manuscript)

On New Year's Eve, Seema and Jack went with Tama and Aurel to a party, a benefit for the peace movement, which continued to oppose the United States' entry into the war. Stalin's pact with Hitler was still in force—Germany had not yet invaded Russia.

Seema chose her dress for the evening with care—it was black with a fitted bodice and a full skirt, with a pink panel down the front. The look on Jack's face told her he approved.

"Let's dance!" he put his right arm around her waist and took her right hand gently in his left. At first he moved slowly, leading her in the foxtrot, but soon he relaxed as he found she could follow wherever he led.

"Do you know that I met your sister and Jerry years ago when I was in the Film and Photo League?" she said.

"Yes, Jerry was in the New Music Society—he was working with Schoenberg then."

As they went on, swirling around the dance floor in the waltz that followed the foxtrot, chatting about common friends and experiences, they realized they had been present at many of the same events for years. Jack had been at Harvard when Seema was still in Boston, and they had attended the same farewell concert by Anna Pavlova, and the same performance by Chaliapin. These discoveries seemed quite magical. When they returned to Windsor Avenue with Tama and Aurel in the early morning, neither one was the least bit sleepy.

Everybody very kindly retired to bed and left us sitting by the fireplace. We sat for a while, and then we decided it was more comfortable lying down, so that's what we did, and it was very natural, on the couch by the fire in the living room. You could see the flames in the fireplace, and Jack came over to me, and he put his arms around me, and we started making love.

Tama remembered looking in the doorway seeing Seema and Jack together with their heads together, reading.

If that's the way she remembers it, fine. But we were not reading all the time.

After it was all over, he had to go home. He was living with his mother, and he had to show his face there. He said he had a wonderful recipe for eggs, and asked what time he could come back and make breakfast.

It must have been dark when Jack walked two miles down the hill to his mother's house on Edgemont Street, but after he had wished her happy new year and started back up in the morning light, did he see the yucca pointing its leaves skyward, or the bougainvillea spilling shocking pink and orange flowers over the white picket fence at the corner? Or was his mind so filled with images of Seema, her eyes laughing up at him, her dark curly hair in his fingers as she fitted her flexible, responsive body to his, that he didn't notice anything at all about his two long walks?

He came back at a reasonable hour, about nine o'clock, and he went into the kitchen and started to make scrambled eggs for the two of us. Pretty soon, my sister Tama came in, rubbing her eyes from sleep.

He said, "Would you like some scrambled eggs?"

She said, "Yes," so he put another egg or two in, and then Aurel came in, and then Joy, and Mother, and then my stepfather Sam. So Jack was standing over the stove, making scrambled eggs for all these people, smiling and laughing and talking.

Nobody said, "What the heck are you doing here?" because as far as they were concerned, he was making scrambled eggs.

Seema's niece Joy was nearly eleven then—she had never had eggs with cheese and walnuts, the way Jack cooked them, and it made such an impression on her that she remembered those eggs sixty years later, when she told me how she first met Jack.

The family stood around in the bright sunny kitchen, holding their blue, orange, or gold Fiestaware plates that Tama bought at the secondhand store, for it was still hard times—Aurel was painting public murals for Roosevelt's Works Progress Administration, not earning much money, and the family was using food stamps. Jack scooped eggs into the plates while Seema stood by, beaming at the man who would be her companion for the next forty-four years.

The next day I had to go back to the Valley. So we said goodbye, and then we started to write to each other.

With Jack, Seema had no need to define or explain her political beliefs. Although he came from a socially prominent family that had once been wealthy, he was wholeheartedly committed to communist causes.

The Weatherwaxes, like Jack's mother's family, the Bryants, traced their arrival in North America back before the American Revolution. Johann Andreas Weiderwachs left the German Palatinate in 1711 with his wife and four children and arrived in New York a widower with two children, his wife and two of the children having died en route. His name was Anglicized, first to Widderwax, then to Weatherwax, and he took up farming near the town of Rensselaer in upstate New York. His youngest son Jacob and his family moved to Michigan; Jacob's son, John Martin Weatherwax, moved from Michigan to Gray's Harbor in Aberdeen, Washington, where he founded a lumber dynasty. At the height of the Weatherwax family's prosperity in Aberdeen, they owned fifty thousand acres of timber, several lumber mills, two logging camps, and two ships.

Jack's branch of the family lost their money in the early years of the twentieth century. His father died when Jack was seventeen, and his mother told him that he was now the head of the family—he was to look after his younger brothers and sister Clara. Jack was torn between his own desire to study and his family responsibilities, which he took very seriously. He went to Harvard for two years, working to support himself, but could not afford to continue. Returning to Washington, he attended the university in Seattle, then started a construction company that failed in 1927 when the lumber mills of Aberdeen closed down.

He was briefly married to Idella Prunell, a writer with whom he wrote a series of children's books. Idella gave birth to their daughter in Mexico and the baby died of dysentery at eighteen months. Jack never saw the child. When Idella and Jack separated, he moved to Berkeley, where his sister Clara was living with her husband.

Jack came to California about '31, and he began to read all kinds of left-wing literature. He was downtown in San Francisco and . . . this heavy, big, black guy stood on a soapbox and started to talk about conditions that existed at that time.

After a while he said, "The police have not given us permission to march—will everybody start walking behind me—I'm going to the Communist Party headquarters."

Jack followed them on the pavement, to see what would happen, because it was all so new to him. He was so amazed that they had the nerve—a whole lot of people joined the march behind this guy—they had the strength and the guts to do it. That impressed Jack very much. So after a while, he went down there to Party headquarters and he offered to help.

They put him to work mimeographing, folding and mailing things, all the little things that had to be done, but nobody trusted him because he told them about his background. His family was very wealthy—some of them were in Who's Who. *He had gone to Harvard, even though he had to work to go there, but they didn't know that, and his branch of the family was poor by that time, but nobody knew that, so they thought he couldn't honestly be interested in the movement. He had to prove himself all the time.*

Jack helped in the San Francisco general strike of 1934 that was triggered by "Bloody Thursday," when ship owners attempted to reopen the docks where the longshoremen had been on strike for months. Of that terrible day, when two workers died, thirty more were shot, and many more suffered from the clubs, gas, and stones of police and strikebreaking goons, Tillie Olsen wrote, "I am on a battlefield, and the increasing stench and smoke sting the eyes so it is impossible to turn them back into the past."[*] Jack would never forget the violence he witnessed against the workers, just as Seema never forgot being imprisoned in Russia as a child.

One of the things that brought Jack and me together was that both of us were involved in the betterment of life for everybody. I wasn't as political as he was—we both worked in the community where we lived but he was more knowledgeable about national and international affairs. We agreed on our basic philosophy, and we did as much as we could together.

Back in Yosemite, Seema picked small branches of flowering dogwood and packed them carefully to protect the delicate blossoms, then she

---

[*] "The Strike," Partisan Review, I, 4, September–October, 1934; reprinted in Jack Salzman, ed. *Years of Protest: A Collection of American Writings of the 1930s* (New York: Pegasus, 1967), 138.

sent the box off to Jack in Los Angeles with a note, "Contraband from the Valley—but I thought you would like these."

After six months of letters back and forth, I wrote to Jack, "Is it all right with you if I come to Los Angeles? I feel that we might be able to have a meaningful relationship and I don't feel we can get to know each other by long distance." He wrote back and said, "That would be great."

I gave notice to Ansel and Virginia that I would leave at the end of the summer.

"There's this man in Los Angeles, and I think he's somebody that I want to know better. The only way I can is by going down there and finding out if it's something I want to do."

Ansel put his arm around her. "I hope everything turns out well, but if it doesn't, come back, your place is here."

Soon after Labor Day, Seema packed her things and moved back to Los Angeles, where she stayed at first with Tama and Aurel. They had moved to a house on Alvarado Street, at the top of the steepest hill in Los Angeles, and Jack frequently walked up that hill to visit Seema.

Reva went straight to the point. "He's nice, Seema, but what does he do for a living?"

"Well, he's paid for his work with the Free India Movement."

"How much?"

"Not a lot, it's movement work. Don't worry, Mother. I can take care of myself."

Reva remained suspicious. She had not forgotten Tama's father-in-law saying, all those years ago in New York, "First you get a job and support your family. Then you work for the Movement in your spare time." Reva retained her conviction, held since her children were small, that Seema was a "softie." She never understood why Seema had insisted on marrying Jim, or why she had left Clarence. Bohemian Chan was entirely outside Reva's frame of reference, and now she and Tama worried together about Jack, while Freda, as usual, kept her own counsel.

I didn't think it was anyone's business but my own, but Tama thought I was strange and close-mouthed.

Jack was doing a program on current events for the radio (KFVD, a Popular Front station), and Woody Guthrie was playing his guitar and doing a program next door. Jack went over to introduce himself, and he and Woody became good friends. This was the period of the Dust Bowl, and the government had these farm projects around Bakersfield, where some of the Dust Bowl people could go and live in fairly decent circumstances.

Jack was on a committee formed to help the Dust Bowl refugees; they organized a benefit party for the government-funded Shafter camp outside Bakersfield, and Woody Guthrie agreed to perform. First, though, he wanted to meet the camp people.

Woody, who had drifted west with people from the Dust Bowl and knew the poverty he sang about from his own experience, had made

fiɢuʀe 32. Woody Guthrie with homeless mother and child, Bakersfield, photo by Seema Weatherwax, 1941. Courtesy of Seema Weatherwax.

some money in New York recording his music. He went straight to a car dealer with his earnings and bought the longest car in the lot, a Cadillac, which he drove out west with his wife Mary and their kids, munching hot dogs and ice cream as they went. They were stopped by police in every town to check the ownership of this fancy car by such a ragtag family.

Woody and Jack and I got into Woody's big Cadillac and we drove to Bakersfield, to the Shafter camp, where Woody played for the people there, and we invited them to a big party that was going to be held in Los Angeles for their benefit.

Just before we reached the camp, we picked up a man, woman, and their baby boy—they were hitchhiking from Oregon. The woman was pregnant with another child. The man had been a worker in a sawmill for twenty years, and he'd got silicosis. He was obviously dying. His cheeks were a brilliant red, like somebody had painted them, and he was very thin. When he got silicosis the owner of the sawmill paid him off with a couple of hundred dollars, and said that was his severance pay. "Thank you, good bye."

At that time he still thought that he could find work, so he decided to come to California where there were jobs, he thought. Of course, if somebody looked at him, they could see that he couldn't last long.

The family was going to a motel run by old friends who had often invited them to visit. Woody drove them to the motel, but there was no welcome for the destitute family there. When the three friends pleaded that the tired travelers be given time to rest before going on their way, the cold-eyed owner reluctantly agreed, and so Woody, Jack, and Seema said goodbye. Once on their way they discovered the woman had left her purse in the car and they drove back to the motel, only to find that the family had left. The owner said he didn't know where they had gone, and although they drove around looking, they were unable to find them. The purse contained a handkerchief with a little twist of coffee grounds in it, a washcloth, and some pennies.

They were a very fine American couple, but there was an absolutely hopeless situation. I photographed them as they were coming down the road.

When they arrived at the camp Jack started to talk to people, and Woody started strumming on his guitar. He sang song after song as people, mostly men, gathered around him. Later, they talked about the benefit concert they were planning in Los Angeles. Meanwhile Seema wandered around the camp, meeting women and children and asking if she could take their photographs. She photographed a little girl about ten years old whose face was covered with freckles and another little girl peering out from the tent where her family lived.

Seema was attracted by the dignified bearing of one of the women and asked if she could photograph her. The woman agreed, and offered to show Seema her first painting, which she had done from memory, of her hometown in Ada, Oklahoma (fig. 33).

The gaunt woman with her crown of braids looks straight into the camera, smiling faintly, holding her painting of hills and fields, people and animals, all the lushness that had disappeared into the dust.

Seema also photographed Woody, his hat tipped back on his head, with his arm around the young camp director, Fred Ross.

Fred was running the camp on the basis of one adult, one vote, including himself. The discipline, the cleanliness, the care of the children and of the people as a whole were fantastic. They had a wonderful community spirit there.

Dorothea Lange also photographed people from the Dust Bowl in the Shafter camp, and Seema said Lange gave a true picture of how people suffered. In her own photographs, Seema said, she focused more on cooperation and survival, celebrating the spirit of the people she met, those who kept themselves clean even while hitchhiking, those who kept house in tents and small metal houses. She photographed some of the people waiting outside of the labor camp, living in makeshift shanties while waiting for an opening in the camp. Their situation, like that of the family on the road, was bleak. To offset the harshness of what they were seeing, the threesome from Los Angeles sang songs.

All the way there and back Woody sang, and Jack sang with him. They composed some songs and they sang all the old songs that Woody knew and they never repeated themselves.

meanwhile, world war ii . . .

We began to hear of whole towns being swept away. It was unbelievable to all of us. Pretty soon after that, the Soviet Union came in fighting.

figure 33. Artist at Shafter Farm Labor Camp, photo by
Seema Weatherwax, 1941. Courtesy of Seema Weatherwax.

The Soviet Union entered the war when Germany invaded in June of 1941; at that time American Communists gave up their pacifism and enthusiastically supported anti-Fascist efforts. The United States remained neutral until Pearl Harbor was bombed by the Japanese on December 7, 1941. The next day the United States and Great Britain declared war on Japan, and three days later, on December 11, 1941, Germany declared war on the United States.

When the United States joined Great Britain, France, and the Soviet Union as allies in the fight against the Axis powers, American Communists threw all their support behind the war effort and those who could enlisted in the armed forces. While American popular support for the Russians as allies grew, suspicion of Communists at home persisted.

The House Un-American Activities Committee was active for years before the United States entered the war, looking into the activities of suspected Communists. Similar investigations were conducted in several states, including California, where Jack Tenney chaired a group known to the Left as the Little Un-American Committee.

This was the backdrop against which Seema and Jack's romance was played out.

Seema finished her last camera sale of the day, to a young soldier who was going overseas. "Why don't you try this one?" she suggested, gently steering him away from an expensive camera.

I just didn't want the soldiers buying stuff they couldn't use once they got overseas, which was not necessarily the policy of the store.

She was working at Castle's, a large camera store on Vine just off Sunset in Hollywood. Now that the United States was at war, American soldiers were coming into the store every day. The work, which consisted mainly of selling cameras and photographic equipment, was easy for Seema and she liked meeting the customers. It was her way of supporting the war effort.

After work she took the streetcar, then walked up the steep hill to Tama and Aurel's house at the top of Alvarado Street. "You can't stand up straight, or you'll fall backward," she told her colleagues at work, describing the angle of the hill. Jack never complained about the climb when he visited her—he quietly suggested that she move in with him.

We started to live together, at his house. His mother didn't like it a bit.

Dora Mabel Bryant Weatherwax, called "Dodie" by her children, came from a prominent Los Angeles family, and her marriage to Clyde Weatherwax was considered a good match on both sides.

The Weatherwaxes were handsome, very good-looking, strong guys, very polite and well educated. Dodie and Clyde were both of the upper class although her family was more genteel. She was a devoted wife and mother—she'd been brought up at a finishing school, and she was taught that you marry, you bear children, and you take care of them. She played the piano, she sang—she had a good life while Clyde was alive.

Jack and his younger sister Clara, both writers associated with the progressive movement, were Dodie's favorite children, and when they moved to California, she left Aberdeen to live near them. She bought a house on Edgemont Avenue in Los Angeles, a lovely, tree-lined street in an affluent neighborhood. A small slim woman with a coronet of white braids, a few inches taller than Seema, Dodie dressed simply and carried herself with great dignity. Her strong moral and ethical beliefs did not encompass extramarital sex, a topic she did not consider fit to discuss, but because she adored Jack and Clara, nothing they did could be entirely wrong in her eyes. She tolerated Jack's relationship with Seema, but just barely.

We right away started to take steps toward getting married.

Las vegas

Seema had never gotten a divorce from her first husband, Jim Lacey. In California, violence or adultery were the only acceptable grounds for divorce, so she went to Las Vegas, Nevada, where you could get an uncontested divorce based on incompatibility. She took a leave of absence from Castle's at the end of January 1942, and left for Las Vegas on an overnight train from Los Angeles, arriving the next morning before the shops opened. As she had time for breakfast before her appointment with an attorney, she went into a restaurant near the station, lugging her suitcase.

"Now let me guess," the waitress said. "You're here for six weeks, hoping the louse won't contest the divorce."

"I'd like two eggs over easy with extra-crisp bacon and a coffee, please." Seema ignored the remark about divorce, but she smiled pleasantly and the waitress grinned back at her.

The attorney had booked a room for her at the Windsor Hotel, and when she finished filling out the necessary papers she took a taxi from his office to the hotel, which was just outside the town center. It was a plain white building, clean and simply furnished.

figure 34. Owner, Windsor Hotel, Las Vegas, photo by
Seema Weatherwax, 1942. Courtesy of Seema Weatherwax.

"I'll be here until mid-March," Seema said to the gray-haired manager, waiting for a joke about divorce, but the woman just nodded and handed her a key.

Once she had unpacked her things, Seema set out to explore Las Vegas.

Only one of the big casinos had been built then. Las Vegas was like a small country town, except that every restaurant and every place of business had a one-armed bandit, a machine for gambling. And of course the bigger hotels had more than one.

The road in front of the Windsor was unpaved, but after five minutes she was walking on the paved main street of Las Vegas, which boasted a post office, several restaurants, shops, a gambling casino, a public library, office buildings, a city hall, an athletic club, and a photography lab. By midday, Seema had obtained a visitor's card for the gym and signed up for exercise classes, continuing the routine she had begun in Los Angeles when she moved back from Yosemite; she also joined the Las Vegas public library and borrowed a stack of books, which she carried back to her room. By the end of her first week she was ensconced in a routine of reading and exercise, and she had made friends with the owner of the hotel, a straitlaced, retired miner.

He did not like women who wore nail polish or eyebrow pencil. He thought they were fallen women, because he'd been brought up in mining towns, and the only women who painted themselves were the prostitutes. Also, many of the women who came to get divorces either came with their boyfriends or they played around—it was an easy town to play around if you wanted to. Well, I didn't play around or wear makeup, so I was a "nice" girl, so he liked me.

One evening he invited Seema to accompany him and his manager to a casino.

"You'll be interested," he said.

They went to the small casino in the center of town, not the big fancy El Rancho on the outskirts.

He walked like a zombie straight to the tables and started playing. I could have done a nude dance in the middle of the room and he would have not known. He was chaperoning me, but from the minute his foot set down in that place he was no longer with it. He was a gambler from the word go.

The manager went off to play the slot machines, and Seema decided she would do the same. She spent five dollars on the machines, then turned her attention to watching her friend at the roulette wheel, marveling at his transformation. After several hours, he came out of his trance and looked around for her. They walked back to the hotel in the cool air of the desert night.

After Seema had been in Las Vegas for a week, her friend Ellen arrived. Ellen was estranged from her husband and she was engaged to one of Aurel's friends, a Hungarian Jew named Ali. Seema and Ellen had planned to go together to Las Vegas to get their divorces; Jack and Ali would join them later and they would have a double wedding. But Ellen was delayed in leaving Los Angeles for a week, and Seema, who had already arranged for time off from work, went on ahead of her friend.

Ellen was from Austria. She was a difficult person in many ways and she had reason to be—her family was killed in the Holocaust. She had already left Austria, but they were wealthy and they thought they were immune. They believed the stories that it was only the troublemakers who were being taken, that the people being rounded up were only poor Jewish people and Communists. They thought, we have money, we have prestige, so they stayed. Of course, the prestiged went in the same way as the others. They were picked up and exterminated. So she suffered from it; she felt guilty that she had survived when everyone else was killed, and she was very neurotic.

This was as close as Seema could allow herself to come toward realizing the horror Ellen carried with her. Seema could not look too deeply into her friend's eyes, because the shadow cast by the camps darkened them. No appetite could be normal, no activity straightforward for Ellen; she wasn't interested in going to the gym nor in reading; but she would sit for hours, watching children at play in the park.

For Seema, who was good-tempered and sociable, the strain of sitting quietly with Ellen grew heavy. She went into the photo lab and asked if they could use some part-time darkroom help for the next month. Yes, they could, and she was delighted to be able to earn some money and have interesting work. She found that she could devote more attention to Ellen when she was not with her all the time, and the next four weeks passed easily.

After a few weeks in Las Vegas, Ellen learned that her husband was planning to contest the divorce. She withdrew her application, as she could not afford a court battle. Ali said he would still come to Las Vegas with Jack for Jack and Seema's wedding, set for March 17, St. Patrick's Day.

Honey: I can send you $25.00 tomorrow or Wednesday, will try to make it tomorrow. Also, $15.00 from Reva, making a total of $40.00. Sorry like the dickens it isn't more, dearling, but that's the works.

Your note of yesterday just arrived. Glad tidings, bells ringing, birds outside chirping, feel good! You haven't much "freedom" left—better run out and spend a quarter at the Casino, or go to another movie or sumpthing (Golly! Mistakes galore in this typing! Ah'm dead-tired, that's why! Just got home from downtown, and have to turn around in 30 minutes to go to Ali's, from whence to a 7:15 meeting of railroad folks about the mag.) Get all the sun you can. It's the best medicine in the world. And remember to eat plenty of salads, and sleep plenty, and sound! (Old Doc Yak, or Jack, spikkin!)

Oh, honey, I'm so glad you'll be finished with that "stretch!" It's awful walkin' around, and talkin' to no-one, and wakin' up in the mawnin yawnin and no-one there! Chrissake! Words ain't no good at all. I can't tell you how I've missed you. Can't write you love letters, 'cause no words can say the thing. They seem so flat, so god-damned meaningless when they're down, I wish sometimes we could toss them all out of the window, and do our lovin' the way nature intended—with all of the senses, including those we use for talking,' just busy a-makin' the loved one happy! And consequently makin' the one doin' the lovin' delirious. And it all goes both ways!—So if you see what I mean in all that, you're good. Expressed simply, it's "To hell with words! Gimme my Seema!"—Gawd. Hurry up, kid!   J

—typescript of letter to Seema from Jack,
dated March 9, 1942

I was married in a soft pink and pale green plaid suit. I didn't want to get married in white, especially before a judge. We weren't having an elaborate wedding.

An older couple who came to Las Vegas every winter and rented a suite of rooms in the hotel had taken a liking to Seema, and they prepared a lunch for the wedding party. Jack and Ali were due to arrive by noon.

Time was going on and Jack wasn't there. Everybody was bothered but me, because I knew Jack by then. I knew he was in the middle of something that had to keep him until it was finished—but they thought I was being jilted.

So the landlord was walking the halls, the manager was walking the halls, and this couple would ask every five minutes, "Isn't he here yet?" Nobody ate lunch except me. Finally, at five o'clock, these guys came in. So everybody got back to normal. I wasn't jilted, so everything was fine. But by five o'clock the judge had already gone home.

They found Judge Marshall's address and went to his house. His wife telephoned the judge, who was playing poker with friends, and he agreed to meet them at the courthouse, where he would perform the ceremony.

Now, Jack was an absentminded professor when it came to ordinary life. Any day that you asked him about from Moses on, he could tell you what happened, but he couldn't tell you if it was my birthday or his own birthday today or tomorrow.

He used to type all the time. He'd move from side to side to look at papers; and he had a special pair of pants that he used to wear for typing. They were wonderful warm pants, but from use they had holes worn in the bottoms. You could see a spot as big as a tennis ball of white underwear on each side when he wore those pants, but since he was doing it at home nobody cared. So he came to Vegas with a suitcase and an overcoat because it was cold that day, and he was wearing those pants. In the suitcase there were three shirts and a couple of pairs of underwear, socks, nightclothes, everything except another pair of pants.

We went to the judge's office, a big long room and the judge was sitting behind a desk at the other end. He said, "Take your things off there," so Jack had to take his overcoat off.

We walked up to the judge, and he said something about the ring. Jack had forgotten the ring. So I borrowed a ring from Ellen.

Then the judge said, "Where's your papers?"

Jack said, "Wait a second, they're in my coat pocket," and he backed up, because he didn't want the judge to see the holes in his pants. This became a ceremonial bird dance—he did these backward steps all the way across the room and got the papers and brought them over, and then the judge asked him for something else, and he did it again. By this time I was ready to explode, but I didn't want to laugh in front of the judge, because he was very serious. He thought I was overcome because I was getting married— but I was overcome because I couldn't laugh. After two of those mating bird dances, we finally got married, and then Jack was able to put his overcoat back on.

They spent their wedding night at El Rancho, the first big fancy casino hotel built outside of town on what would become the Strip; the next morning they went down for breakfast.

They called it a Hunt Breakfast, like they used to do in England before going hunting. They had everything, meats and cheeses and fishes, a big fancy breakfast. That was where the people with money went, and Jack was the only man there in an overcoat.

SUMMONED

They drove back to Los Angeles after breakfast. Jack had received a summons to appear before the Tenney Committee on March 19, two days after their wedding. State Senator Jack Tenney's California Joint Fact-Finding Committee on Un-American Activities was investigating allegations that Jack was a member of the Communist Party. No wonder he arrived late to his wedding, wearing his old trousers with holes in the seat—he was scrambling to prepare for the hearing!

The next day Seema went with Jack to the courthouse. Jack was escorted to the front of the room where the committee sat, and Seema was left to find a seat among the spectators. When she sat down, several of the male spectators made jabbing gestures with their middle fingers in her direction, and one man with a large florid face cupped a hand under his elbow and balled his fist at her. She felt her stomach muscles tighten, and she looked straight ahead.

From her seat at the back of the room she couldn't hear what was being said up front. There was a drone of male voices, and she saw Jack sitting alone at a table, his back to her, facing another table where white men in suits consulted their notes. The men near her continued to make angry gestures in her direction. They mouthed words at her: "Commie," "Red," "Scum."

She didn't know how long it lasted—it felt like many hours—but finally Jack rose and walked back toward her. They left the court silently, and they walked several blocks before Jack put his arm around her and said, "It's all right, my dear. I told them I am a Harvard man, a Christian Scientist, and a Mason, which, as you know, is simply the truth. That's all I told them, and it had to satisfy them."

It was a while before Seema stopped trembling.

Now that the United States had entered the war on the same side with the Soviets, public investigations of Communist activity had cooled considerably. Jack was not a Party leader and so he had received the same advice as any of the other rank and file who were called to testify.

"Don't give them an opening, and don't answer any of their questions." That was the word—there was no time for individual briefings.

All kinds of people were called before that committee—if anybody heard you saying, "I don't like the way the mayor is running the city," you were already subversive, so you would be called up. You considered it an insult if you were not called before it—that was a joke we had.

Jack was not blacklisted officially, but after that, when he sent some of his books out, they were returned with a note saying, "We are not able to print it," that sort of thing.

Seema would not be specific about Jack's or her membership in the Party.

Jack was working with different groups during the war; he was the head of the Consumers' Committee for Los Angeles and he did a lot of public service things; and he was with the Free India Now movement. He was writing.

Within the movement, one did not ask one's friends if they were Party members. Historian Marge Frantz said that when she left the Party in 1956 she did not know whether or not her own sister was still a member. Seema said sometimes she belonged and sometimes she didn't, but anyway, what difference did it make?

I have always worked for causes I believed in, not for any party or politician: equal pay for equal work, women's rights, racial justice, these are what matter. The basic philosophy of the CP is that there is an oppressed class and oppressors, and that has to change.

Both Seema and Jack were either in or closely associated with the Communist Party during times when it was dangerous to admit to such an association and when the Party asked its members to keep a low profile. The anti-Communist atmosphere Seema experienced personally in the 1940s and 1950s was still very much alive for her half a century later. Others of her generation shared her fears; the hysterical persecution that lumped together Communists, fellow travelers, liberals, and progressives imprinted a habit of silence in many who never gave up their beliefs but simply went underground with them.

Seema's sense of secrecy went back much further than the 1950s, to the first Red Scare that climaxed in the notorious Palmer raids of 1920, when foreign nationals suspected of subversion were rounded up and deported. These "foreign nationals" included some of Seema's friends and relatives, and when she arrived in Boston in 1923 government repression of left-wing radicals was firmly in place.

Seema summed up her political work by saying that she and Jack supported struggles they believed in: organizing farm labor, working for racial justice, and promoting freedom of expression and cultural exchange; when their approach differed from the Party, they followed their own path. The fellowship they felt with the Party provided them with a large extended family, including many actual family members and old, dear friends. When friends left the Party, convinced that the Communist experiment in the Soviet Union was a dismal, terrible failure, Seema and Jack did not stop seeing them—they simply agreed to stop discussing divisive issues.

Okay, so I'm not saying it was perfect. The Soviets did make mistakes galore, and one of the reasons why I wasn't always there was because I didn't agree with it. One mistake they made was not allowing intellectuals to leave.

They invested money and time to train people to be useful, but in the end, if the people were not satisfied, they should have been let free. There were a lot of things that I believed that they did wrong, you see.

Even though we disagreed, I still felt their basic line was good. Their way of doing it was wrong, but I feel that the basic philosophy in the Soviet Union probably was correct.

I rejoined the Party or stayed with the Party because there were enough wonderful things that I believed in that they were doing. They were very dedicated people. I didn't agree with everything they thought, but it didn't make them bad people. It's like, Is marriage the best institution? It's not perfect, but it's the best we know, so we stick with it.

IN DODIE'S HOUSE

"They're here, Dodie."

Seema, elegant in a black satin suit, stepped down from the screened back porch into the garden. Dodie's silver braids gleamed under the flowering peach tree as she stooped in the late afternoon sun, picking a few final flowers to supplement the bouquets she had arranged throughout the house. She nodded at Seema and, straightening her collar, followed her new daughter-in-law inside.

Everything was ready in the large living room, where a fire burned brightly on the hearth. Dodie had insisted on giving the wedding reception for Seema and Jack at her house, and Reva, who worked long hours at her slipcover business, gratefully agreed. It was a small gathering, consisting of close family and a few friends.

Jack couldn't brag enough about Seema, saying to his brother, "I'll tell you the secret of being happy. Marry somebody who is kind and has a good sense of humor," and he gave his new wife a hug.

Dodie provided hors d'oeuvres.

The food was okay if you weren't too hungry and if you were planning to eat afterward. But it wasn't lavish. If my family had made the food, you wouldn't have needed to eat afterward.

The atmosphere was cordial, as they had all come together in celebration, but there was an obvious distance between the two very

figure 35. Wedding reception for Jack and Seema, Edgemont Street, Los Angeles, 1942. Courtesy of Seema Weatherwax.

different families, most evident in the puzzlement with which Reva regarded Dodie.

Mother was young enough to be [Dodie's] daughter. They had nothing whatsoever to talk about, in a deep sense, you know, so they were polite, but there was no embracing, because Dodie did not go in for that except for her favorite children. There was never any hostility, but mother couldn't grasp who this woman was, and she didn't make any big attempts because it was a barrier that they couldn't get over. They came from completely different worlds.

Seema, always sensitive to inequality, felt her mother-in-law's coolness in marked contrast to Dodie's warmth and interest in Jack and Clara.

She and Jack and Clara were a threesome, like triplets. And nobody else really counted for Dodie. She would read up on any issue that Jack and Clara were involved with, and if she agreed with it, she would get involved, too. They were her life.

Happily for Seema, Dodie often invited Clara and her husband, Jerry, for dinner.

CLARA

Clara Weatherwax was known in progressive circles for her novel *Marching, Marching*, which won the *New Masses* prize in 1935 for the best American novel on a proletarian theme. She had drawn a vivid picture of the lives and struggles of lumber workers in her hometown of Aberdeen, Washington, but her writing career was cut short by crippling arthritis, which came on suddenly in her mid thirties.

Clara was still walking when Seema and Jack were married, but as time went on she would be confined to a wheelchair. As her hands stiffened, she became unable to write.

Despite her illness, Clara and Jerry decided to have a child. Their son, Mark, was born a few years after Seema and Jack married. Clara's illness progressed, and she died in the mid 1950s, less than a year after Dodie's death. Then, a few months later, fourteen-year-old Mark disappeared into the ocean while swimming, in view of his horrified father, and his body was never found.

In those early days they all gathered around Dodie's table, formally set with water and juice glasses, dinner plates and side plates for bones, two forks and two spoons at each place, and finger bowls, and they talked about supporting the war against fascism. Dodie was a staunch supporter of all that Jack and Clara did.

"The Free India movement scored a great triumph, Clara. Jack had the brilliant idea of hiring an elephant to walk in the War Bonds parade. They hung banners on one side of the elephant saying 'Buy War Bonds' and on the other side saying 'Free India Now.' It was the hit of the parade—I wish you had been there to see it." Dodie glowed with pride in Jack as she offered second helpings of the roast.

figure 36. Clara Weatherwax and Jerry Strang, Seema and Jack,
Los Angeles, ca. 1943. Courtesy of Seema Weatherwax.

*Dodie always gave small helpings. Never too much on the plate at once.
Her salad was a leaf of lettuce on a plate with a slice of avocado and a section of grapefruit. I was used to lots of vegetables in salad—in my family,
when we had salad, we ate salad!*

*Once Clara told me she thought Dodie didn't treat any of her in-laws
well. She saw that about her, but she still cared for her.*

*We were very close. When she was so ill and you talked with her on the
telephone, you couldn't tell there was a thing wrong with her. Her voice
was all, "Now what did you do today? How are you? How's everybody?"*

Just like nothing was wrong. She would never talk about how she was lying there with a canopy over her legs because she couldn't stand the weight of the sheets.

Living in Dodie's house, Seema found that the only space where she could really relax and feel at home was the bedroom she shared with Jack. Dodie did all the cooking and housekeeping, and Jack had his assigned chores. "He took out the garbage and filled the water glasses."

One day when she came back from work and was heading down the hall to their bedroom, Dodie looked up from her book and said, "Jack's asleep. You'd better not disturb him."

Seema turned, her hand on the doorknob. "He's my husband, Dodie. I think he'd like to see me." And she went into the bedroom.

"It's not working out, Jack," she said later that evening. "We need a place of our own."

Jack nodded. It was hard for him to believe that his mother was not as warm and loving to Seema as she was to him, but he wanted to make this marriage work. That September, a house belonging to friends in Laguna Beach fell vacant, and they had a chance to live there for six months. Seema left Castle's camera shop and took a war job wiring circuits for planes in a factory at Laguna Beach; Jack settled down to his writing, driving up to Los Angeles several times a week to attend his meetings and check in on his mother. At forty-one Jack was too old to enlist—instead he volunteered to work with the rationing committee of the city of Los Angeles, and he continued his work with the Free India movement.

married Life in war and peace

We'd never had a chance to be alone and we loved Laguna. We had a beautiful little garden and a fireplace, it was really ideal. If you went very close to the corner window you could just see the water—it was blocks and blocks away.

We were both working. Jack had to be in Los Angeles a lot of the time, and I got a war job. We went dancing together; we had good contact in every way; lovemaking was easy and good.

Outside their honeymoon house with its white picket fence, the war continued. Communists were united with the rest of the country in the fight against fascism, and Seema performed her war job with enthusiasm. Each afternoon she went out through the garden gate and off to work, where she showed the same competence and dedication she had always shown in the darkroom.

There was a little factory in Laguna Beach that made parts for airplanes. It was a subsidiary of Douglas Aircraft, and I was hired to work there on the night shift. I'd come in and there were these women sitting with a little jig in front of them, about a foot by six inches, and they would have these wires. You were to draw the wires around the little pegs in certain patterns. Most of the workers were local women who were not used to earning a living. They would put the wiring on the same little jig, day after day, month after month, and they loved it.

I felt capable of doing more than that, and so did another woman, so she and I were given the new jobs and the rush jobs. Some of them were very difficult. One time they had a cable about the length of this room that had to be covered with a plastic cover, like tubing. We had to find a way of putting that tubing, which was pretty tight, on the cable from one end to the other. We had to solve all these things, so it was very interesting, and I got a nice citation when I left.

Seema's family and friends were inspired by stories of the heroic Soviet struggle against the Germans. Unable during the war years to correspond with her cousin Liza in Moscow, Seema would later learn that Liza's husband was killed early in the war, and that except for one cousin, their entire family in Chernigov disappeared.

You heard all these horror stories and you couldn't believe that it was happening. Chernigov was overrun by the Nazis. Cousin Tamara, she was the daughter of Dveira, the one that had the school that I went to, she turned up in Moscow, years later, and they said that she was very vague— they couldn't find out what happened to the other members of the family.

After six months, Jack and Seema moved back from Laguna Beach to a furnished apartment in East Hollywood.

I got another job that was part of my war effort. We were x-raying the metal parts that had to go into airplanes. They looked like what I think bars of gold should be like—we were supposed to photograph all four sides to see if there were any cracks or flaws in the metal. Well, some people would be talking, so they'd photograph this side and they'd still be talking, so they'd photograph that side again, and then the second and the third. Again and again, people would be distracted and they were not photographing all four sides. I couldn't stand seeing that kind of carelessness. I went to the foreman and he said, "We'll manage very well without you interfering."

We had to enter the building with a special card for security, but when we finished our work it was piled outside in a yard where anyone could walk in and do a little damage to those things before they went to the airplanes. I used to say to these women, when the bosses wouldn't listen to me, "Do you realize that your own husbands or sons could be flying planes that will crash because these might be defective?" But there was nothing we could do.

They were building a new darkroom where I was supposed to develop the x-rays. That's what I was hired for, but by the time the darkroom was ready they fired me. It was one of the few times I ever was fired from a job. They said there was someone already slated to do that work so they didn't need me. They didn't say it was because I was too particular, but I knew exactly what it was.

Seema was not alone in her concern. A few years later Arthur Miller's play *All My Sons*, about a businessman who shipped defective cylinder heads to the Army Air Force causing twenty-one planes to crash, would win critical and popular acclaim on Broadway and was made into a Hollywood movie.

> *"It's nothing you can see with the naked eye,*
> *but it shows up in the x-ray."*
> —from the movie *All My Sons*, directed by Irving Reis, 1948

the united nations

Very soon after I was fired from that x-ray place, the war in Europe was over. Jack and I went to San Francisco because he was a press representative to the first United Nations conference.

Before the war was officially over, Jack and other idealists began preparing to attend the first United Nations gathering, held in San Francisco in 1945, immediately after Germany's surrender to Allied Forces and while the war with Japan continued. The atmosphere was ebullient, full of plans for the newly emerging peace.

We all knew that the United States government would rather have had the Soviet Union as an enemy than as an ally. But we didn't mention that. This was before they started working on the treaties, so we were all hopeful.

Seema and Jack stayed in a small hotel in San Francisco for most of the month-long proceedings. Jack, who wrote for *India News* and the *People's World*, had obtained a press card good for all events; Seema was able to attend all the general sessions and she found her way into many of the special sessions as well.

Sometimes I would use Jack's card to get in, and then I'd come and give it back to him and he would go off to another session. I took notes for him on the sessions he wasn't able to attend.

Every hour was full. The different delegations hosted parties, and that's where you got to meet and talk to people. I learned about rich and poor nations from these parties. The Balkan countries were too poor to host a reception, but the Arabians put on feasts.

At one point, Seema took pictures of two of the Soviet delegates, a man and woman, beaming at her, then she noticed two press photographers watching her. Fearing they would ask for her credentials, she packed her camera away and left, not wanting to be banned from the rest of the proceedings.

The *New York Times* published a special edition that appeared daily during the United Nations conference.

I thought, the New York Times—*that's where you get all the truth. I had an excellent memory, and I often took notes on what was said. Then I would read the* Times. *They would get 99 percent right, but they would add or leave out one little word and that made all the difference. I saw it time after time. I learned—don't trust any newspaper article until you check it out.*

Jack sent a postcard to his twelve-year-old nephew Jackie, whom he had never met. Postmarked May 16, 1945, with a picture of the Spanish

Civil War monument in Union Square, the message gives a sense of Jack's hopefulness, also his schoolteacher tendencies:

> The city is filled with guests from abroad: Arabs, Panamanians, Chinese, Russians, Egyptians, Hindus. There is a theatre (free) open only to United Nations delegates or press and their guests. The United Nations Charter is being written. It will be the *political* foundation of the peace, while Bretton Woods, with its big international currency stabilization fund and bank will be the *economic* foundation of the peace. Meetings on the Charter take place in the Opera House, which is not shown in this picture.
>
> —Uncle Jack.

Scrawled in the margin, in a darker ink, "Saw [U.S. Secretary of State] Stettinius today; had a half-hour talk with Masaryk yesterday."

Jack knew a wealthy woman in Los Angeles who had family connections to Jan Masaryk, a popular war hero who was the Foreign Minister from Czechoslovakia. She wrote a letter of introduction and Masaryk welcomed Jack and Seema warmly. While he and Jack discussed the possibility that the Czechs would receive aid from the United States, Seema sat quietly, listening to the messengers who came into the hotel room from time to time and spoke to the Minister in Russian or in Czech, delighted that she could understand a good deal of what was said.

Masaryk's dream of the reconstruction of his country was crushed when the Soviets vetoed Czech acceptance of U.S. aid under the Marshall plan. Three years after his meeting with Jack and Seema, having remained at his post after the Soviet takeover of Czechoslovakia, Masaryk died. It has never been clear whether he committed suicide or was thrown from his office window.

For Seema, who retained her idealism about the U.N., the event was memorable as another opportunity to meet interesting people, a party with a great purpose:

I went to a lot of lectures; I managed to go to all the cocktail parties and meet the delegates, and so I saw the United Nations at its formation.

CROSS-COUNTRY AGAIN

Jack carefully documented all the treaties produced at this conference, and he put them together in a book with the title Peace Key. *Then we went to New York, and Jack tried to see people about his book.*

On their first night on the train, as soon as they turned off the light Jack fell asleep, but Seema felt trapped in their small sleeping compartment—it seemed to her that she would suffocate.

Fumbling for her clothes in the dark, she dressed and went to the lounge car where she read for a while, then she decided to explore. She walked through the narrow corridors of the swaying, racketing train until she found the compartment where the porters sat. They invited her to join them and offered her coffee, which she sipped while chatting with the men.

In the daytime, when the beds in their compartment were made up into seats and the window shades were raised, she slept in her seat.

figure 37. Jack with James Ford, Golden's Bridge, New York, photo by Seema Weatherwax, 1945. Courtesy of Seema Weatherwax.

In New York they stayed with Seema's cousin Reva and her husband, James Ford. He was the first African-American to run for Vice President of the United States, sharing the Communist Party ticket with William Z. Foster in 1936 and 1940. Seema proudly showed me a newspaper article with a photograph of her cousin-in-law.

Jim was wonderful, easy to get along with, and he welcomed us as if we were brothers and sisters. If you went to New York you had to go to their house—he was the macher—*you don't understand Yiddish, do you? That's "maker," or "doer."*

The summer of 1945 was a tense time for American Communism. Major Party conventions were held in July and August to establish postwar direction and deal with a split in party leadership. Earl Browder, who had helped create the Popular Front and favored continuing to work in coalition with other progressive groups, was on his way out, and William Z. Foster was working to reassert his leadership with a doctrinaire Party line. James Ford was removed from the Party's national board in July and made head of internal security in a general shakeup that must have preoccupied him during the whole of that summer, but he was a genial host to Seema and Jack.

Jimmie did most of the cooking. We went to their summer cabin in Golden's Bridge, in Westchester County, and we stayed there for one or two nights; then we went to their apartment in Harlem. It was a nice apartment, but you had to be careful about cockroaches.

In Harlem Seema and Jack climbed the stairs of the elevated train station, turning their faces from the sooty blasts of the train as it pulled in to the platform, then they rode the racketing subway downtown, two naive Californians hoping to publish a book of treaties aimed at world peace in the midst of a political maelstrom.

To Seema, the arguments she heard in her cousin's apartment in Harlem resembled the arguments she was used to hearing around any dinner table where Aissen family members gathered.

We went to see Howard Fast—he was a left-wing writer, and we met William Z. Foster—he said Peace Key *was a good book, but Jack said to me afterward that it was too bad he didn't take time to read it thoroughly. Everyone said nice things about the book, but in the end we had to publish it on our own. Jack didn't get disappointed though—he just went on doing things.*

Seema and Jack went to Washington, D.C. as tourists. On their first night they went to the wharf on the Potomac, where they had been told they would find the best restaurants in the city. It was a warm evening and people were strolling along the river. There was a spicy scent of cooking coming up from the lower level of the wharf, and Seema and Jack went down and waited for a table. All the other people in the restaurant were black.

Soon the waiter came over, deferential, but looking very troubled. He said in a gentle voice, "We can't serve you here. I think you will be more comfortable upstairs."

They went to the upstairs restaurant, where a sign said "Whites only," but they could eat very little.

It was such a shock! I still had ideals. Here was Washington, D.C., the seat of our country, where everybody was supposed to be equal, and we couldn't even eat where we wanted because of the race problem. I didn't know it would be that open, right at the capital.

For their train ride home, knowing that she wouldn't be able to sleep in a bunk, Seema tried to get a refund on her sleeping car ticket and buy a cheaper seat on a coach. The ticket agent said he couldn't give her a refund, but he offered her a coach seat in addition to her sleeping car place, which she accepted.

They stopped to see the sights in Chicago, where they stayed in a noisy hotel full of soldiers traveling home from the war. When they boarded the train again, Jack escorted Seema to her coach seat, where they discovered that she was the only woman in the car—all the rest were soldiers. By sheer good fortune their old friend Hank Shires, an artist whose work they both admired, was sitting in the seat opposite Seema. Still in uniform, he was on his way home. Jack sat down to chat for a while.

As it got late Jack said he would go to his compartment and Seema suggested that he leave his hat on the seat next to her, so that no one else would sit there. Eventually a porter came and offered Seema a seat in another coach, where there were other women and children, but she pointed to Jack's hat and said, "My husband . . ." The porter nodded and left.

"I suppose he thinks Jack is off getting drunk in the bar," she said to Hank, who grinned back at her.

"I have to tell you this, Seema," Hank whispered. "When you went to the bathroom some of the guys came over and asked me how I got a woman so soon!"

There was no one sitting next to Hank either, so the two friends slept well in their double seats. The next morning Seema woke and went to the restaurant car to meet Jack. She found a seat in the restaurant, but there was no Jack, and when she went to look for him she discovered that there was no car beyond the restaurant. All the sleeping cars had been disconnected during the night; as the train was so long they had divided it in half.

Every time the trains came into a station, Jack and I would rush out and embrace on the platform. Then we'd go back to our separate cars. We were on separate trains for two days and two nights.

Like old times at yosemite

On our way back, we went up to Yosemite for recreation.

"Jack, wake up." He was alert immediately and joined Seema at the window of their little cabin. "There's a bear out there." They peered out into the darkness of early morning to see the lumbering shape prowling under the trees. Seema had gotten up to use the bathroom, a short distance from their cabin, and she saw the bear as she walked back.

It was like old times. They stayed in a cabin at Yosemite Lodge and walked the Valley trails. They ate dinner with the Adams family and Jack held forth on the United Nations. Ansel was interested in their views on the issues of racism and discrimination, as he had photographed Japanese-Americans interned at the Manzanar camp the year before, photographs shown in a controversial exhibit at the Museum of Modern Art and then published in the book *Born Free and Equal*. He was now attempting to launch a project on African-American education, without support for this provocative work from his usual patrons.

After a week at Yosemite Jack returned to Los Angeles, anxious to press on with his work preparing *Peace Key* for publication. Seema

figure 38. Mt. Lyell, photo by Seema Weatherwax, 1945. Courtesy of Seema Weatherwax.

stayed for another two weeks in the Adamses' small guest cabin, next to the cabin where she had lived during her working years there.

That was the time I took the longest, hardest hike of my life. There were five of us: Ansel and his son Michael, a young man who was helping in the darkroom, and another young woman and I. We went by car to Tuolomne Meadows, and we slept overnight there, then we hiked from the Meadows up to the foot of Mt. Lyell, nineteen miles, on a trail over logs across rivers.

We carried our bedding, our sleeping bags, food, and between the five of us we were carrying several cameras, big ones; one of them was Ansel's 8 x 10. I had my camera too, heavy, even though it was a small one, and I took some good pictures of Mt. Lyell (fig. 38).

It was a very strenuous climb, just a footpath over rocks, ten thousand feet where we started at the meadows going up to eleven thousand feet. I enjoyed it, but the very last fifteen minutes I was suffering from lack of air, and when we finally got to the foot of Mt. Lyell my heart was beating very very fast, and I had to lie down flat to recover.

I was already over forty, and I hadn't done any hard walking or climbing for a number of years. The young woman who was with us kept stumbling and falling on the rocks—she was much worse off than I was, because she was a city girl and I had been used to walking on trails. The two young men were very able, and Ansel was like a goat—he could climb anything. So it was a wonderful and very hard experience.

HOLLYWOOD

For the next eight years Seema balanced her political and social activities with regular exercise at a gym and her job at Castle's, where she was rehired after the war. By now the store had its own darkroom, so she divided her working time between selling cameras and photographic equipment and developing and printing film.

She enjoyed sales. Many of the NBC people from the studio across the street came into the store, and Seema liked meeting and bantering with them, although several times she got into trouble with Mr. Castle, the owner, for not being sufficiently obsequious to the stars.

One time Costello of Abbott and Costello came in. He always had a bunch of followers and he was a pain in the rear end. He came right up to the counter, and said, "I want . . ."

I said, "Hello, would you mind waiting in line? I'm waiting on this customer and then after I take the other person I'll be glad to take care of you."

He got red in the face and yelled, "I want service!"

He reported me to Mr. Castle, who came to me and said, "What do you mean by not taking care of him?"

figure 39. Exploring the World, Lakshmi Singh, Los Angeles, photo
by Seema Weatherwax, 1942. Courtesy of Seema Weatherwax.

*I said, "When you are at the counter, you do what you think is right,
and I will do what I think is right."*

*I called him Mr. Castle most of the time. Occasionally we got together
for a party and then I'd call him Andy, but on the job I called him
Mr. Castle.*

Seema could surely have found much more creative and interesting
work after working with Ansel Adams for three and a half years, but she
settled for the job at Castle's because her focus was on Jack. As she had
done since 1923 when she first came to Boston, she earned her living as
needed, without thinking about her own creative potential.

She identified herself as a working person, not as a creative artist. Having witnessed the early struggles of great artists like Dorothea Lange and Imogen Cunningham, Seema was practical about her need to earn a living.

After I married Jack, I thought, here I am going to be doing mainly darkroom work, taking photographs for my own benefit. Maybe I had ideas that I wanted to do special things with children and photography and the world we lived in, a book of that sort. I thought about that, but then I thought, Jack had all this talent. I felt that he was able to reach the public better than I could, and so I supported him. I knew that you never made money doing things like that.

But I could have let people know that I was capable of doing other things, because many times people treated me as if I didn't know anything. I was the secondary character. I don't think that was correct—I should have asserted myself a little bit more.

It would be many years before Seema would assert herself as a public figure. But at Castle's, Seema was clear about her status and needs as an employee.

I quit several times while I was working for Castle's because I didn't like the conditions. Mr. Castle wanted to cut our pay, and he wanted to have me work on Saturday. I needed time to myself.

I'd say, "I'm sorry, I can't do it. I will be glad to train a new person." I trained somebody three times. Two times he called me back within a week or two. Each time I would say, "Whose conditions? Yours or mine?"

He'd say, "Yours," and I'd say, "Okay, I'll be back, Mr. Castle."

On one of her breaks from Castle's she did some portrait photography of children. She took candid photographs of a young mother and her baby, the mother feeding the child, the child crawling around and playing with her toys. The mother was pleased with the results, but she commented that Seema charged more than Austin's, a local portrait studio.

Austin's took family pictures in a portrait gallery, wearing fancy hats and doing fancy things and amusing the kids so they would laugh, and I wasn't doing that—I just was following the children around doing what they would do naturally.

After several experiences like this Seema gave up the idea of running her own business.

I didn't have a darkroom but I thought, other people use their bathrooms and kitchens and so on, so I tried it, but it was very uncomfortable. Trying to do it on the commercial level, it was absolutely no good. Without having a regular darkroom, I'd have to clean up and put the chemicals away after each session, because it was in an ordinary apartment. So it was too much work for something that was not rewarding.

It wasn't a question of Jack restraining me, or being unable to talk to him about it, it was just that it never occurred to me. I knew that I could always work for somebody else, and I had enough other interests.

In 1944 and 1945, despite pledges of the AFL and CIO not to strike until the war was won, wildcat strikes broke out in the auto, steel, and rubber industries. People who had been grateful for any job during the Depression were now organizing to demand better working conditions and better pay. Once the war was over, strikes erupted all over the country, supported by the progressive movement, including the Communist Party. In Hollywood, where the main union was controlled by the American Federation of Labor and corruption was rampant, the Screen Writers Guild and the Conference of Studio Unions attempted to organize a movement that would better represent the workers' interests. Seema and Jack were on the side of the workers, of course, and Seema took her camera to the picket line (fig. 41).

We were involved with the Hollywood strike of 1945, in which goons and all kinds of strikebreakers were brought in. They pushed people around, trying to get them out of the picket line. I was careful to take photographs only when no one was noticing me.

This young woman here was our friend Jimsie Porter. She was given a very good job reading scripts, because of her family connections [her father was Bruce Porter, a San Francisco artist]. The day that she arrived was the first day of the strike, so she put down her invitation to come into the studio, and picked up a placard to walk with the strikers. She was staying with us at that time, and a couple of days later she came home white-faced and shaken. She said, "Now I know how false it is to say the

Communists use violence, because we were walking peacefully in the picket line and the goons came in and started using their sticks, breaking people's heads."

a LittLe pLace in santa BarBara

Their young friend Jimsie Porter had inherited quite a lot of money, which was an embarrassment to her. While the Hollywood strike was under way, Jimsie asked her friends Joe and Witz Biddle if they would go to Santa Barbara and sell her family house there. In the winter of 1945–46, the Biddles, who were also good friends of Seema and Jack, invited the Weatherwaxes to join them in the large, beautiful house, and Jimsie came up for visits.

It was a little place, it had eight bedrooms with a bathroom in each bedroom, and a couple of other bathrooms for the help, you know, and stuff like that. The four of us were rattling around up in this mansion on "Nob Hill."

Jimsie didn't want any part of the house; she didn't want to inherit anything. She had so many wonderful things to inherit and she just wanted to get rid of it all.

The four radical friends had a wonderful time on the sculpture-dotted grounds of Jimsie's Santa Barbara mansion. Jack was preparing *Peace Key* for publication by the Bryant foundation that he, Dodie, and Seema had established. He felt justified in his efforts when he received a letter from the U.S. Secretary of State, Cordell Hull, who said he carried *Peace Key* with him to every international conference.

While they were in Santa Barbara, Seema worked for several months in a photography lab. On foggy mornings when she set out for work, the town and the ocean were hidden from view, but when the sky was clear she had a panoramic view over golden hills and the red tiled roofs of the town below to the ocean, navy blue in the winter sun.

The key to the maintenance of world peace, however, becomes clearer to more people daily. That key is Big Three Unity [the United States, Great Britain, and the Soviet Union]. A new world war is not inevitable. Friendship between the two greatest

figure 40. Jimsie Porter's house in Santa Barbara, photo by
Seema Weatherwax, 1945. Courtesy of Seema Weatherwax.

powers, the United States and the Soviet Union, is not only possible, it is necessary. Big Three Unity as the basis for a successfully
functioning United Nations is attainable . . . The path of the dis-
ruptors and liquidators of the allied coalition is the path of war-
in-the-making: the road of Big Three Unity—the people's
road—is the road of peace-in-the-making.

—John M. Weatherwax,
Peace Key, part I, Treaties, Conferences, Agreements

ORGANIZING

After five months in Santa Barbara Seema and Jack returned to Los Angeles, where they rented another furnished apartment in East Hollywood, on Melbourne, off Vermont. Seema resumed work at Castle's, and she and Jack reentered their busy Los Angeles life of work and organizing. After her workday at Castle's Seema returned home to cook dinner for herself and Jack, who had been writing at home or attending meetings during the day. Then they would go out to meetings, or go square dancing, or Seema would get on the phone to help organize some event.

If there was a struggle going on, I would join that struggle. If it was a labor struggle, if they were having a march downtown, which the labor

figure 41. Hollywood strike, photo by Seema Weatherwax, 1945. Courtesy of Seema Weatherwax.

unions did, I would join that march, either with a labor group, a church group, the farmworkers, whatever group I was closest to at that time.

If there was any tabling to do, to save somebody's life or get somebody out of prison, I would stand at the corner of the street, at Santa Monica and Vermont, where Ralph's grocery store gave us permission to have a table and have petitions on their lot at the side.

By this time, Seema had given up on serious photography.

When I would go out with people, I used to take my camera with me. We'd be driving along, and I'd see something good. "Oh, that's great, back up a little bit, I want to take that."

People would hop out of the car and say, "Where do you want me to stand?" I'm exaggerating, but it was almost like that.

I said, "I don't want you to stand anywhere, I want to take that mountain or that tree or whatever."

"But you want to see the size."

I stopped taking my camera with me when I went out. It's that simple. Most people were involved in snapshooting, and I was not. So I thought, forget it, it's too complicated.

As the Red Scare intensified, the House Un-American Activities Committee focused on Hollywood: in 1947 and again in 1951 actors, writers, and directors were subpoenaed and asked to name their friends; those who refused were blacklisted and some were sent to prison. Seema was discreet about her political activities when she talked to the people at Castle's, but she never tried to disguise her beliefs.

Bob, the manager at Castle's, was a good friend. We disagreed about a lot of things, for example health care, because the words socialized medicine *scared him. But every time it came to voting, he'd say, "Seema, whom are you voting for?"*

I'd say, "Why do you want to know? We don't agree about my ideas." He said, "You always pick out good people."

So I would tell him, and he would vote that way. It was very funny.

At this time I was the chair of our Communist group. A young man came to live in Los Angeles in our area and he joined the Party. His name was Charles. We never knew for sure if that was his right name or not— at that time some people did use false names.

Anyway, Charles and his wife and little child lived in the neighborhood and she became pregnant. Charles was a schlemiel, *he was always having things happen to him, because he was inept. He got a job in a kitchen, so he'd scald himself with water; he got a job doing carpentry, so he fell down a ladder. He wasn't a* schlemozzle—*that means luck is against him—he was just inept, so they were having a hard time making a living.*

We organized food and help for the family, and I decided to crochet a nice blanket for this new baby.

Then came this headline in the paper, spread across the front page, "Communist cell exposed," and it said my name and Jack's name, and they quoted me, with language that I never used. I went into work, and there was Bob.

I said, "Did you notice the front page of today's paper?"

"Well, there's some article about some Communists or something like that."

I said, "Just glance at it again," because I knew he would later on.

He said, "Oh, your name is there."

We'd worked together about five years by that time. I said, "Bob, can you believe that I would talk that way?"

"No."

"The rest of the article is full of the same kind of lies. You can see for yourself that the person they're describing isn't me."

He said, "It's true, there's no way that you would talk that way, under any circumstances."

"That's true, so they're distorting what I would say, which means they're probably distorting the Communist stand on things, right?"

"Yes."

"All I wanted was for you to know about it."

I never had problems with any other person. Andy Castle, the owner, was the guy I was really worried about—he once said, "Communists and atheists are lower than a snake's belly." I don't think he read the paper and understood that it was me.

So anyway, it came out that Charles was a stool pigeon. He was getting some minimum sum from the FBI, like $75 a month, for his information.

Of course we had a confrontation with him, and from that time to this I never knitted another baby blanket.

Of all the organizing Seema did in her years in Los Angeles, her most vivid memories were of cultural events. She and Jack hosted meetings between visiting Soviet artists and African-American artists, and they were the first to bring the Harlem artist Charles White to Los Angeles, before his work was known on the West Coast.

On February 27, 1948, Paul Robeson gave a concert at the Second Baptist Church in Los Angeles, sponsored by the Civil Rights Congress. Because of his open support for the Soviet Union, Robeson was black-listed. No longer allowed to sing at regular concert venues, he was still appearing at churches.

Somebody in the church group decided, he's a Communist, forget it, he can't come to sing here. Well, Jack was a member of the Baptist church.

He went to this church group that had said no and he said, "Look, this man has a beautiful voice. As Christians we have to give him a space and freedom to sing his songs."

Jack had a silver tongue, so he won. Paul Robeson did sing, and he was wonderful. You felt like throwing your arms around him and embracing him, he was such a warm human being.

The hall was packed to standing room only and we had all the biggest strongest men in the movement as bodyguards. They stood against the wall, ready to save him if they had to. I was there in back, watching to see if anything was needed. It was the first time I had heard Paul Robeson sing in person, and when he opened his voice, my feet started to tingle. I'm telling you this, of this time so many years ago, and I can still feel it, such a strange sensation, you hear music through your ears but this was through my feet, that's how his voice was. It was so powerful, once he'd opened his mouth, I could hardly stand any more, my feet were so alive.

COMMONWEALTH AVENUE

On weekends Seema and Jack went around the neighborhoods near theirs, distributing pamphlets and selling copies of the *People's World*,

figure 42. Hattie Brown, photo by Seema Weatherwax,
ca. 1983. Courtesy of Seema Weatherwax.

the popular West Coast Communist newspaper. One of the neighborhoods they visited was in East Hollywood, east of Vermont, about eight
blocks square and centered on Commonwealth Avenue. The one- and
two-story houses were set back from the street, with yards where children played and people sat out on their front porches in the evenings.

*It was not Watts, not a black ghetto, but practically all the people who
lived there were black. There were some large families, like Odetta's, who
lived in three or four houses. These were modest homes, not expensive. About*

one-third of the people owned their own homes and the rest were renting, and they were charged higher rents than whites for comparable housing.

People were still coming from the South, looking for jobs. I knew daughters of slaves, and one woman whose mother was the second wife or mistress of a plantation owner. My friend remembered this white man coming to her house when she was a child and saying, "It's good to be home." He paid for all the children's education, so my friend had finished high school, which was really something then.

Both Seema and Jack were strongly interested in the struggle against racism, which had gained new momentum after the war, as African-Americans who had fought for their country in the segregated armed services were in no mood to take up second-class citizenship when they returned. The Communist Party was in the forefront of the fight to end lynching and segregation, still firmly entrenched in both custom and law.

At that time, interracial friendships were unusual. Seema and Jack had gotten to know the people on Commonwealth when Jack joined the Baptist church that many of them attended about a mile away in Echo Park, where there was another black neighborhood.

There were Baptists in Jack's family, so he entered that church in good faith even though he was not religious. The minister said, "If you become a member of this church and are here on Sunday, people will start to believe what you say." And so Jack was a member of that church for twenty-five years—later he became a deacon.

I used to go to church about once a month. At first the minister asked me to join, but I told him, "I don't believe in the divinity of Jesus and I don't want to repudiate my own people."

I asked if he was comfortable with me being there, and he said, "If you keep your mind open, you can think of trees or anything that is beautiful and good on this earth, and as long as you have that feeling, you're welcome in the church."

The Party said that was terrible. They said, "Seema, how can you go to church and stand there and help them sing hymns?"

There's no question that from way back the Communist Party did more for justice against racial discrimination than any other group, but they did not have enough respect for the groups they were trying to get together with, because they were so sure that they had the correct line that they expected others to follow them.

Seema and Jack continued to distribute their pamphlets and newspapers even as anti-communism intensified.

I didn't carry a roll of papers under my arm, like I did before. I'd carry a paper or two in my purse and I visited. We went to people that we knew wanted the People's World, and they'd say, "We're having fish for breakfast, fish and cornbread, come, sit down and eat with us."

As she spoke of fish and cornbread for breakfast I heard a musical lilt in her voice, evoking African-American speech rhythms.

We got to be good friends with a man called Coleman. His daughter Maryann and his son-in-law had bought a big house on Commonwealth Avenue, and at the back of their lot they built a garage with an apartment on top and another apartment on the side, both for rent. Coleman said to Maryann, "Why don't you ask the Weatherwaxes?"

Some of the neighbors said, "Why the heck do you want to have white people here? You should rent to black people."

Maryann said, "Look, we're all supposed to be brothers and sisters and they're on our side."

In Watts and other East Los Angeles neighborhoods there were whites who had stayed put when black people moved in, but Seema didn't know any other whites who had deliberately moved into a black neighborhood.

I loved our apartment. You went up a flight of wooden stairs to get to it, and it was airy and bright and nice. We'd been living in furnished apartments, so we had to start from scratch. We went out to buy the essentials—a bed and a secondhand icebox, because we couldn't afford a refrigerator, and a secondhand stove. Then before we bought anything else, we had a housewarming party.

We borrowed bridge tables and folding chairs and we had forty-two people to dinner. People were sitting on the bed and the toilet and the bathtub and on the stairs outside. I had two meats, ham and something else and drinks—it was a fantastic party. Later on we went out and bought a few other odds and ends, so the house was comfortable with old furniture.

Seema and Jack lived on Commonwealth Avenue for five years (1949–54), a period of time she remembered as exceptionally rich. They invited square dance callers to come each week, and everyone in the neighborhood joined the dancing in the big paved area in front of the garage. There were potluck dinners and celebrations of all kinds, to which they were regularly invited. Maryann, their landlady, hated to cook and Seema hated to clean, so twice a week Maryann cleaned and Seema cooked for both households.

One of their neighbors was Odetta, a young woman of nineteen when the Weatherwaxes moved to Commonwealth. Her mother worked cleaning a local theater to pay for her daughter's singing lessons. Odetta was classically trained but she was beginning to sing blues and folk songs, working as a live-in servant to support herself. Seema remembered first hearing the great singer at a party, long before she was well-known.

Her voice and her presentation were wonderful, full of power. I thought, "My god, why isn't she known more?"

Seema continued to work at Castle's Cameras; Jack worked at his various writing projects and committees; and they organized in the neighborhood.

Soon after we moved in, we started the East Hollywood Interracial Council, and at first we worked on a local issue—Safeway didn't have any black employees in their stores in black neighborhoods, so we protested, successfully. Then we worked on some national issues, like jobs, housing, and social justice. We'd set up tables, handing out pamphlets and asking people to sign petitions.

One evening Seema and Jack attended a benefit organized by Dean Ella Matthews, who was the head of a small, nondenominational, neighborhood church. She introduced them to a young woman named Hattie Brown, who had just moved to Los Angeles from New York. Hattie was looking for a place to live—she had been walking around the neighborhood, looking for an apartment, and she had gone up and down Hoover Street, one block from Commonwealth, where she was told again and again, "We do not rent to black people," "No Negroes allowed." The Weatherwaxes knew of a small house for rent on Commonwealth—Hattie became their neighbor and one of Seema's closest lifelong friends.

Hattie filled in some of Seema's memories for me, emphasizing the many family connections in the neighborhood. The Johnson family owned a big house on Commonwealth and the small house behind it which they rented to Hattie—they were related to Odetta and her family, and Hattie remembered going with four or five other young people to visit Odetta where she worked at a white family's house on Hoover Street. They would go on Friday or Saturday evening, when Odetta's employers were out and she was looking after the children, and Odetta often sang for them as they sat together drinking wine.

Seema and Hattie told me many stories about their neighborhood women's group, which functioned as a consciousness-raiser for each of them in different ways.

We formed a group of eight to ten women who used to get together once a week, and we called ourselves a sewing group. I hate to sew, so I used to iron. Somebody would sew something for me and I would iron something for them. Another woman would bake a cake.

We were working women. There were some civil servants who worked for the government, but most of the women did household work for white people. They used to tell stories that were amazing and wonderful, and we laughed ourselves silly half the time. They would tell about their real feelings about being servants in white houses, about people saying, "This maid of mine is like a member of the family. The only thing is she doesn't eat with us in the dining room when we have guests, then she has to eat in the kitchen."

One of the women told us how her employer said to her, "We're going to use this nice china so be very careful, do one at a time."

Well, this woman had the exact same set of china in her house, and she felt like saying, "You stupid thing . . . don't assume because I'm black and a servant that I don't know how to handle good china."

They were breaking it down to everyday, small things that were demeaning in their daily life, in relationship to the people they worked for. I thought that was very important for me to know. We know about the big things, about people being stopped on the street and being beaten, but we don't realize these little things that go on all the time, that make a person feel bitter or mad or downcast.

Hattie said that the sewing group was a place where they ironed, cooked, and talked about world affairs, beginning with and branching off from their own experience of being treated as if they were less than human by the white people they worked for. They heard about a young black man who was picked up by the police because he was caught in a white neighborhood, and they organized groups to go out and put up signs and distribute pamphlets on his behalf, taking care to avoid the police themselves. "We would put up signs on walls and run like hell," Hattie said. "We were young and we were going to change the world." She spoke about setting up tables to hand out leaflets—"Seema and Jack were always there, at all our protests against wrongdoings to the black community. There was no one like them."

Seema was clear about the way she and Jack insisted on supporting the black community to find their own issues, despite pressure to bring in the Party agenda:

We said no, we go with what the people want, we do not bring our program in there. If they want a table for the Scottsboro boys, we support that. If they want to free Tom Mooney, we support it, but we do not come in and say, "You have to support Tom Mooney because he's unjustly in jail." And some of the Communist Party members would come to the next meeting of the Interracial Council and say, "We've got to get more active on getting help for Tom Mooney." And I said, "That's completely wrong. This group, knowing the facts, has to make up their minds what they want to support and what they're able to support. We can tell them if they don't know the ins and outs of any situation and they're interested in knowing, that's another story. But not to take over and say we're going to do this."

Hattie remembered a Passover seder that Seema organized, held in one of the black homes on Commonwealth, where a rabbi spoke about the plight of Jewish children in refugee camps in postwar Europe. Hattie brought her five-year-old niece to the seder, all dressed up in her pink Easter dress and white shoes, and when little Diane heard about the sufferings of the Jewish children she ran to the rabbi, sobbing, to give him the fifteen cents she had in her purse. The rabbi put his arm around Diane and comforted her, so effectively that soon after, when Hattie went looking for her niece, she found the child playing happily in a tree which she had climbed, even though she was wearing her best clothes!

Seema had heard about a progressive young rabbi at the university who was known for his interest in the black community, so she invited him to come to a seder.

Everybody was amazed that he was so outgoing, just like everybody else. We always tried to bring different groups together. Jews and blacks should be working together, we thought.

Hattie said that the rabbi also collected money to help Ethel and Julius Rosenberg, who were in prison for the crime of espionage. Their case attracted attention and sympathy all over the world, but although at least in the case of Ethel there was no conclusive evidence, the pair were executed in 1953. The memory of that event caused Seema's mouth to quiver when I mentioned it, nearly half a century later.

The Cold War red scare was at its height, but the people on Commonwealth were used to closing ranks to protect their own. Soon after Seema and Jack moved into the neighborhood, the FBI came around, asking people about their new neighbors.

The woman across the street, Ida, was a matriarch. She was a very nice person and a very bad dancer who had no sense of rhythm. She broke all the stereotypes, but she had a wonderful time square dancing with us, and everyone used to avoid being her partner!

Ida was naive and nonpolitical. One day the FBI came to see her about us. She said it wasn't a good time for her and they said they would come back the next day, so then she talked to one of the men who lived on the street who was politically hep.

He said, "Ida, what do you think about where the Weatherwaxes stand on jobs?"

"Oh, they're very good."

"How do you think their thinking is on having equal rights?"

"Very good."

"So what are you going to tell those people when they come tomorrow? Why do you want to even talk to them? Everything you say will be held against the Weatherwaxes and they might go to jail for what you say."

The next day, when the FBI came, she said, "I've nothing to say to you."

Commonwealth was a safe haven for Seema and Jack during the scary years of the 1950s when Party leaders were indicted and jailed, many Party members went into hiding, and many others, in the Party and out of it, lost their jobs and were blacklisted.

Jack and I were a problem to the FBI as well as to the Party, because we had people in all areas who were friends. We had the church people sticking up for us, we had our black community sticking up for us, and Jack came from a wealthy family who were all good, staid Republicans. The FBI had bigger fish to fry. They had hundreds of top-level people in the motion picture industry, and we felt that we were too small fish to be bothered with.

A lot of people stopped attending meetings, but the rest of us carried on as usual. By the time of the Rosenbergs there were people organized all over the place. We would talk about what we could do to support the people being sent to jail and how we could help people to stay out of jail. We drove some people to a place where they would be vacationing for two months to recuperate from a cold in the head, because they were in more danger than we were. We didn't want to actually hide out, we just had to be more careful.

One day I was home alone, and these two well-dressed white men knocked on the door and said, "We're from the FBI."

We had been told that they had no authority to force their way in or arrest you. They could only make a report and then let the police do the rest.

They said, "Can we spend a minute or two talking to you? It won't take long, we just want to know a few things."

I said, "I have nothing to say to you. So please leave."

They came back the next day again.

I repeated, "It doesn't matter how many times you come back, I still am not interested in talking to you, so please don't bother me anymore."

And they never did. Because they knew that I was not going to break down.

Seema was tough when the FBI came to her door, but when a young woman she and Jack had befriended would no longer speak to her, then she felt vulnerable. It was that memory that surfaced when she spoke of the loss of freedom that she experienced in the 1950s.

One day—I hadn't seen her for about three months—here is this woman with a baby carriage coming toward me and she started moving slower and slower. When I got to her, she was standing there shaking, absolutely shaking. I said, "What's the matter?"

She said, "I have to go away, I can't see you." And she went away, shaking. The next time she saw me coming she crossed the street with the baby carriage. She was afraid to be associated with me if I was a Communist.

Immersed in community and family life, Seema had put aside her camera, but when her friend Sir Lancelot, a calypso singer from Jamaica, needed publicity pictures, she agreed to take them, although she had never done work like that before.

One summer she was asked to help some friends who were running a progressive camp for children in the mountains south of Los Angeles. There was a mix of races at the camp—some of the children on Commonwealth were given scholarships, and a son of one of Seema's friends, an African-American boy named Chuck, was a counselor. The children ranged in age from about eight to fifteen.

The older kids were very bored, so the couple asked me if I could help them out weekends. It was a volunteer job. I taught them the rudiments of photography.

There were six to eight kids at the most. We had box cameras that I brought, and the camp directors provided a darkroom. We went out in the woods to photograph and then we'd go back and develop and print.

The first time the kids were in the darkroom I heard a sort of rustling. They were old enough to want to play around with each other, so I said, "Okay guys, cut that out!"

They said, "But it's dark! How can you see?"

"I've been working in darkrooms long enough that I know what you're doing. If you're interested in photography, stay, if not, get out!"

I'm sure they thought I had extra special vision. Anyway, I was able to fool them because they stopped. We did all kinds of fancy things, like expose emulsified paper with leaves on it or flowers. It was fun and it kept them busy for hours.

Looking back from the vantage point of her nineties, Seema said that some of the best years of her life were her forties and fifties, when she was married to Jack, living a fully engaged social and political life, dancing and hosting parties. She also spoke with great pleasure about her eighties and nineties, when she was living alone in Santa Cruz, blossoming into independence.

figure 43. Seema and Jack, Edgemont Street,
ca. 1955. Courtesy of Seema Weatherwax.

figure 44. Seema and Jack, 1965. Courtesy of Seema Weatherwax.

Her sixties and seventies were more difficult, for she had to face mortality, her own and others', as she had not done since her father's death. The first small signals of changes to come arrived early.

I was working at Castle's, and I had always been cold, you know, I would come in sweaters when everybody else was in shirtsleeves, and all of a sudden I'm standing there with sweat dripping off the end of my nose. My friend Bob, the manager, used to kid me, "Are you still cold?" He of course knew what was going on.

She had smoked cigarettes since she was sixteen. When she was in her late forties, her physician took her hand as she was leaving after her annual lung x-ray and said, "I want to say good-bye."

Startled, Seema asked why.

"I don't want to see you anymore," he replied. "If you continue smoking, one of these years the x-ray will show something, and I don't want to be your doctor then."

She went home, threw her package of cigarettes in the garbage, and never smoked again. But three decades of smoking had aggravated her chronic bronchitis, which grew worse each winter. Remembering her experience with Dr. Lovell, the naturopath who had cured her Metol poisoning, she asked around for an alternative healer.

Cecilia Rosenfeld was a homeopathic doctor and a lot of people swore by her. So I went to see her and she was absolutely wonderful. She started me on a diet and homeopathic remedies and slowly but surely I got over a lot of physical things that had been wrong with me through all these years. I began to feel well.

As she moved into her fifties, Seema's full life was touched again by illness and deaths in the family. In 1954 Jack's mother died.

Jack was very very upset about Dodie's death because he loved her so much, but she was going downhill for the last few years, and he knew that it couldn't be forever. He was able to accept her death better because he felt we were doing everything that could be done.

Dodie left the house on Edgemont Street to Jack, and he and Seema moved there from their apartment on Commonwealth, which was only a few blocks away.

Reva's second husband Sam also died in 1954. Seema and Jack decided to divide their eight-room house into two apartments, so that Reva could live in the back and still be independent.

They kept their large living room and dining room in the front of the house intact, with its fireplace, polished oak floors, and built-in china cupboards, perfect for the many gatherings they hosted. The walls were hung with framed photographs by Ansel Adams and Edward Weston and artwork by Diego Rivera, Charles White, Hank Shires, and other artists they came to know through their political work. A small

figure 45. Seema and Jack, 1980. Courtesy of Seema Weatherwax.

breakfast room was converted to a library, lined from floor to ceiling with bookshelves, and it had a bed for overnight guests. They made an eating space in the kitchen, kept one bedroom for themselves, and converted the garden shed out back into an office for Jack, which was also lined with bookshelves and filing cabinets.

For Reva's apartment, Jack designed a wide-windowed living room to replace the old screened back porch, and Chan Weston, who had become a family friend, did the concrete work. They joked that Chan's concrete foundation was sufficient for a ten-story building. Later, Chan tiled Jack and Seema's new bathroom.

It took him about three months to build that shower. Chan would be sitting there beside the bathroom door and you'd walk by and he'd say, "I'm working it out." When it was finished it was a beautiful shower, pink and all the tiles fitted, but for three months we couldn't take a shower in our own bathroom.

By this time I didn't feel anything bad, and Chan didn't either, except later on he said, "I was a damn fool to let you go!"

After they divided the house there was no laundry room, so Seema continued a tradition she had begun with her friend Hattie when they lived on Commonwealth. Encouraged by Jack and Seema, Hattie had enrolled as a student at nearby Los Angeles Community College, and each Saturday the two women filled Hattie's little Volkswagen with laundry and set off together for a sociable morning of laundry, shopping, and lunch.

In those years Seema belonged to a health spa, where she swam and worked out in the gym. She had loved acrobatics and rope work ever since her school days, and this was a way to keep fit after her long hours of laboratory work. When the spa offered half-price memberships to family, Seema convinced Hattie to join.

Hattie was the only black woman in the place. She and I went up to the desk and I said, "I'd like a half-price membership for my sister."

The woman at the desk looked at Hattie and she looked at me, and she didn't know what to say. So Hattie got her membership for half-price.

Also in 1954 Seema finally left Castle's Cameras to take a new job with Frank Holmes and Weststrip, where she first worked at slide duplication and later was moved to filmstrip production. This was demanding, stimulating work.

When you make a filmstrip you are telling a continuous story with stationary exposures on 35mm film. Some of our filmstrips were religious, some were medical or educational, and some were just straight advertising. The point was to join these separate pieces of information, which were on color film, black-and-white film, artwork, posters, anything you could photograph and print so they told a story. You had to have a script, like you would for a motion picture.

At first I was just sitting at the camera and I shot the stuff. But after a while the person would come to me and tell me what they wanted, with all the material they wanted to include, and we would write the script together. Eventually I was put in charge of the department.

During the thirty years that Seema and Jack lived on Edgemont Street after Dodie's death, their lives were filled with people and projects. They had a dog, Thor, a stray that Dodie took in and passed on to Seema and Jack when she couldn't take care of him; several cats shared the front porch with marauding raccoons. There were meetings, parties, benefits, concerts, and picnics in Griffith Park, held near a stream, under shady trees, with white cloths spread on picnic tables and an abundance of rich food.

meanwhile, tama . . .

In 1943 Tama, Aurel, and Joy had moved to a large house on Isabel Street, in Highland Park. Seema first heard about the house from their friend Earl Robinson, the composer who wrote "Ballad for Americans" and "Joe Hill," both unofficial anthems of the Popular Front.

We had these good friends David and Bea Arkin and Earl Robinson and his wife Helen. The two women were sisters. David and Bea were the parents of Alan Arkin. They always wanted Alan to play his guitar at our parties and sing folk songs—he bored us all to death, and then he became this wonderful movie actor.

Jack and I were drinking tea with the Arkins and the Robinsons, and the Robinsons were telling us about this house they had bought that used to belong to Zane Gray and then to Charlie Chaplin. It sounded such an exciting house—Earl loved it, but Helen didn't want to live in it—it was too primitive. She wanted a modern house where there was good plumbing.

Seema called Tama and Aurel, who made an offer as soon as they saw the house. It was redwood, with a slate roof and chimney, set on a half-acre lot, with fruit trees and a view of the hills. An immense living room

figure 46. Frank, Tama and Aurel Leitner with Joy, Isabel Street, Los Angeles, ca. 1946. Courtesy of Seema Weatherwax.

could hold one hundred and fifty people comfortably, with a huge fireplace and a beamed ceiling, three stories high. The Robinsons sold it to them at a good price, on the single condition that they hold progressive benefits there, a condition they accepted happily.

There was a stage in the living room, where Aurel kept his easel and paints when they were not entertaining, and another stage outside, added by Charlie Chaplin when he lived there, so there was plenty of room for concerts. The dining area was half again as large as the living room, and they had a big picnic table to accommodate all the guests who stayed with them. They kept open house all the time, and Tama said she never knew exactly who was staying.

Aurel was master of ceremonies at the many benefit concerts and parties held in the Zane Gray house. Dalton Trumbo and John Howard Lawson (members of the Hollywood Ten who later served prison sentences because they refused to cooperate with the House Un-American Activities Committee) were frequent visitors; folksinger Pete Seeger, cellist George Neikrug, and many other musicians and performers came to help raise funds, first for the strikers and then for the defense of the Hollywood Ten. It was as if the Left in Hollywood were one huge extended family. It was impossible to distinguish political from family circles, and gregarious Jack fitted himself easily into the family scene.

AND REVA . . .

Reva was happiest when surrounded with family and friends, and she loved cooking for their parties and picnics: *forschpei* (appetizers) of chopped liver with onions or grated fresh turnips with *schmalze* (chicken fat) and *gribenes* (chicken crackling); borscht, cold and hot, chicken soup; brisket of beef cooked with lots of onions, vegetables, noodles; *kugel* (noodle pudding) and *strudel.* Her granddaughter Joy said Reva was the "glue that held us all together."

Reva had gotten over her initial mistrust of Jack, and by the time she moved to Edgemont they were good friends.

Mother used to feel that she wasn't up on anything unless Jack visited her every day and told her about what was going on in the world.

Jack interviewed Reva, now in her eighties, about her life, focusing on family, work, and radical activities. She told him how she smuggled pamphlets to workers when she was a child, organized benefits in Leeds for the Bolshevik revolution, chased brick-throwing Menshevik hooligans, and struggled to earn a living for her family after Avram died.

This was one of Jack's many projects, mostly collaborations. In the early 1930s he carried a letter of introduction from the Russian filmmaker Sergei Eisenstein to the Mexican muralist Diego Rivera. Jack

figure 47. Reva, ca 1946.
Courtesy of Seema Weatherwax.

had been interested in Mexican culture since the time of his first marriage, when he had lived briefly in Mexico; Rivera and Jack worked together on a project to publish an illustrated edition of Jack's English translation of the *Popul Vuh*, the sacred book of the ancient Quiché

Maya, but Rivera never completed the illustrations.[*] Later, Jack corresponded with artists from the Taller de Gráfica Popular, a group of radical artists in Mexico City, and he collaborated with one of them on two filmstrips using the art of the Taller.

The house was often filled with artists and students. With his wide-ranging interests in history, mythology, and popular culture, Jack became a local resource for students from Los Angeles Community College.

Jack was a fund of knowledge—he could remember dates from way back, let's say, in the tenth century—he didn't always remember what happened in the twentieth century in his own life—but he remembered all the other dates. So people knew that if they went to him with a question he could either tell them or he could look it up for them.

One of Jack's long-term projects was a series of educational pamphlets on African and African-American history, which he published through the Bryant Foundation. He had managed to ferret out little-known information that convinced him of the injustice and irrational basis of racism. His printer was Oneil Canon, who had been educational director of the Communist Party in Southern California and ran a print shop near Watts with his brother. Oneil first met Jack and Seema during the founding of the Progressive Party in the 1940s, when he invited Jack to lecture at some of the forums and classes he organized; later he founded the Paul Robeson Center to house Jack's extensive collection of African-American books and portfolios.

> The overwhelming majority of the original founders of Los Angeles were Negroes.
>
> This submerged, hidden, suppressed *fact* (for fact it is) is well-embedded in the archives of Mexico, in the earliest records of Los Angeles, and in the writings of scholars and historians of long ago.
> —John M. Weatherwax, *The Founders of Los Angeles*, 1954

---

[*] For a description of this project, see Lucretia Hoover Giese, "A Collaboration: Diego Rivera, John Weatherwax, and the *Popul Vuh*," *American Art Journal*, Vol. 39, nos. 3–4, 2–10, 1999.

Although Seema sometimes felt burdened by Jack's obsession with writing and publication, she believed wholeheartedly in the importance of his work. In Jack she had found the lifelong partner she had been seeking—they were friends as well as lovers, carrying on lively discussions about Seema's work, Jack's writing, their various political and cultural activities.

Money was a divisive issue. Seema hesitated to write checks to pay their bills, for fear Jack had overdrawn their account with philanthropic or publishing expenses. She sometimes came home from work to discover that Jack had just written a check to an artist friend who had come asking for help, ostensibly to feed his family.

That was one of the things that we had serious disagreements about. I said, "I can't work to support this guy's drug habit. I can work for a cause, or I can work for us to do things that are useful, but I don't want to work for that." But I had no choice, actually. We had a joint account, and when Jack's heart would bleed too much he would give the money.

They were in complete agreement about their political work: Jack was secretary of the National Association of Colored Women.

This was a women's civil rights organization, and there were strong black women running it. Jack was the only man involved, but he was only acting as secretary. There was another woman who actually taught kids to not like whites, and I had a real run-in with her at one point.

She had a chip on her shoulder—whites were no good at all, except, some of her best friends were white, like us. She wrote a play about discrimination and had a bunch of us come to act it out. I took the part of the devil, the white woman, and the rest were young black women. By the end of the rehearsals the young black kids were crying, because the woman who wrote it had so much hate coming through that they couldn't take it. She would say, "You've got to say that with feeling," and then she'd bawl me out, she'd say something against white people to me.

One day she said, "We should have a little talk, why don't we discuss what we've been doing." So I said, "I know that we white people do things that are harmful, we admit that, but you have to understand that we're doing it out of ignorance. So teach us, but don't slap us down each time we open our mouths and try to say something. When you say it with hate in your voice, we can never learn. Neither can the young people here learn if the only way they know is to say we're all devils."

So, she listened, and she tried to correct it. Several years later we were talking with a bunch of people, and she said, "The reason Seema and I are friends is because Seema came out openly with me and told me how she felt and we're good friends now." And it was true.

Seema chaired a neighborhood branch of the Party, called a "club," taking on added responsibility as Party membership declined. At one meeting, she sat in one chair to open the meeting, moved to another chair to give the treasurer's report, then moved to a third chair to give another report, dramatizing the need for more participation.

By the 1960s the American Communist Party had lost most of its support, as old members had left in droves following Krushchev's revelations of the Stalin years and the Soviet invasions of Hungary and Czechoslovakia, and younger people were attracted to the New Left movements that emerged from the civil rights struggles and the newest wave of feminism. Seema and Jack remained loyal to their local group of activists.

In both cases [Hungary and Czechoslovakia] I felt I could not make a judgment because I never felt that I knew the facts properly. Most of the information came from the capitalist newspapers, and I felt I was on the outside looking in, not feeling happy about it, but not saying I won't go along with it, because I didn't know enough to take a stand. I felt unequal to understand the situation, so it was my own lack. I wasn't clear on every subject, no more than any other human being.

I was never a theoretician, but I liked people and I knew how to get them going. After practically every meeting we used to go out and drink coffee and talk and have a good time together, getting to know each other—this was not the usual thing. I was very flattered because Rose Chernin was in my club. She said it was fun to be there, and yet you got the same theory and people went out and did the work.

When Kim Chernin published *In My Mother's House*, Seema, who had looked forward eagerly to reading about her old friend, felt that Kim betrayed her mother by questioning the value of her life spent in service to the cause of Soviet communism. "She broke her mother's heart," Seema said, and although I pointed out that the book presents a very different perspective on Rose's reaction, Seema was adamant. The underlying issue, for Seema, was a daughter's loyalty to her mother's beliefs. In Seema's family, the need for solidarity was a matter of survival.

age

As she neared sixty Seema had again to cope with illness—this time Jack's. For the next two decades, in her sixties and seventies, she would face stress and suffering as her closest family—first Jack, then Reva's husband Leon, then Reva and Freda all became seriously ill. These would be the most difficult years of her life, and yet she emphasized to me that they were also full, rich years, as she kept up her old friendships

figure 48. Jack with Thor, Los Angeles, photo by Seema Weatherwax, 1965. Courtesy of Seema Weatherwax.

and formed new ties. Imogen Cunningham, whom Seema always regarded as a mentor, called whenever she was in Los Angeles and the two women compared notes on their lives.

I thought she was old when I met her. She was seventy-nine then. When Imogen was in her nineties, she said to me, "I hate to be old, because I can't do what I want to do."

"Well, what are you doing?"

"I'm getting my papers in order for the Archives, and I'm teaching two classes, and I'm doing a little bit of printing," and she started to go down the list.

I said, "Imogen, you're making me tired!" That's exactly how she sounded. You can't help but enjoy a person like that, you know. She was active to the end of her life.

And so was Seema.

I was acknowledged in the Movement as a mover and shaker like I am here in the NAACP. I was very active with the Unemployed Councils that were run by leftists, way into the '70s. This was people who had been working and were thrown out of work because of the labor situation. There were three or four in the Los Angeles area—I belonged to one in the Echo Park area which was mainly Latino people, mostly Mexican-Americans who had some training. Some of them were welders, some of them were carpenters, but then came no work, and they were thrown out. They thought it was because of their own inability to handle things.

I didn't speak Spanish and I was the oldest one there. I was in with the group because I was able to talk about the Depression, when professors and everybody else were on the street selling apples—this was the same kind of situation. It was the system that was causing them to be out of work, not their own inability.

We wanted to raise money. I was in touch with a machinists' union, Machinists and Aeronautical Engineers, one of the most progressive locals in Los Angeles. They had a wonderful hall and I got permission to have a gathering in that place. The officers of the union came to me afterward and said they were inspired because we had so many different groups, Mexican-Americans, black people, white people, everybody all working together, singing together.

Well, later on we were going to have a meeting of all these groups together, and the Communist Party chair of the district wanted to have it on the East Side, because she happened to be Latina. On the East Side it would be too narrow, it would just be Mexican-Americans, and a few people would drift over, whereas here they accepted us, not as Communists but as unemployed people of all backgrounds, and this was exactly what the party policy was.

I said, we're always talking about having ties with labor. This union would love to have us there—it would be a fantastic thing if we all came and met here, in the center of Los Angeles.

Everybody thought I shouldn't fight with the big brass, but it was a matter of principle. I had a real battle with her about it. In the end I won.

After that, when they had big labor marches, I was given a cap with Machinist's Union on it, and a banner, and I walked half the time with the Machinists and half the time with Farm Labor.

Jack kept up his hectic work pace, writing, doing organizational work, publishing his pamphlets about African and African-American history for children, and, most strenuous of all, traveling in the Southwest for his work with the Hopi people. Seema was convinced that the hardships of these travels worsened Jack's health problems.

Jack printed a newspaper, so he was asked by that tribe of Hopis to come and help them out when they had special meetings, to take notes and put what they said into this newspaper. At least three times he took that trip. You had to go through Navajo territory to reach the Hopi territory, and it was kind of a dangerous thing. They always went one or two cars together for escort, because there was fighting going on between the two tribes. Jack used to go up there and stay two days. A couple of times some of the men came down and stayed at our house, when they had to see people in the Los Angeles area. I remember coming home from work and there were men sleeping or resting all over the living room floor.

The week after the last time Jack went up there he got this fibrillation. I think it was too much for him, because they ate food he wasn't accustomed to, and sleeping on the ground, being cold, being tense, sitting on the ground for hours at a time, probably helped to bring it on. It got acute, to the point where he had to go to the hospital.

When Jack was hospitalized in 1965 following his first heart attack, Seema was in the midst of a fierce struggle at work. The International Association of Theatrical and Stage Employees (IATSE) had been trying to unionize Frank Holmes and Westrip, and when the company resisted the attempt, the union set up a working picket, as they were not yet allowed to go out on strike. Seema along with the other employees was working her full shift and also walking the picket line when Jack collapsed and was hospitalized at Cedars of Lebanon, near Edgemont Street.

For the last five years, Seema and Jack had found tenants for their part of the house on Edgemont and they rented an apartment in San Fernando near Seema's work. Seema arranged for their move back from San Fernando while juggling the demands of the union, her job, and visiting Jack twice a day. When Jack came out of hospital, their lives had been altered, but still they did not slow down.

From then on it was living with something hanging over our heads. We still kept on doing a lot of things. We had friends coming over; we had study circles; we had reading circles; we had just fun circles; and we visited other people a lot too. All this time he was writing on Afro-American history, and he was quite an authority on that subject.

But when Jack got sick, I became aware of the fact that we were all mortal, and I was conscious of the time we had together. I started to think about whether it's better to have things or to have good health. I sold six or eight of Ansel Adams' pictures, and I sold some of Edward Weston's pictures, because we needed money—we didn't have enough medical coverage—and then we started selling our Diego Riveras.

Jack, who didn't sleep well, got into a habit of writing in the middle of the night. Seema would leave a pot of spaghetti sauce for him, and all he had to do was heat the sauce and cook the spaghetti—she often woke to hear him typing or clattering pans in the kitchen and she went back to sleep reassured that he was okay. In the morning she might find a poem he had written for her, lying on the kitchen table.

The union had promised to find Frank Holmes workers new jobs in the movie industry if their organizing attempt failed. It did fail, and in 1965, at the age of sixty, Seema learned another new skill, printing copies of color motion picture film. She was the only woman doing that work at that time, and, even more important for her, she was finally a union member. When she retired in 1970, IATSE gave her a gold card, normally reserved for people with twenty years of union membership.

She was proud of her union gold card, which represented the extraordinary esteem in which she was held.

The woman who appears in family photos from that period was gray-haired and stout, like a kindly grandmother (fig. 44)—at the same time she was working in a motion picture laboratory, holding her own among the men in a notoriously macho industry. She wore glasses, bifocals at first for her presbyopia, then trifocals because of her work in filmstrips. She had lost some weight on the diet Cecilia Rosenfeld gave her, but then she gained it back. She'd stopped going to a gym for regular exercise when they moved to San Fernando, then Jack's health prevented them from going out dancing.

It just crept up on me until one day I realized, I'm really heavy! I'm not just a little bit plump. We did a lot of entertaining and going out and you get careless, so after a while I thought, "Oh well, what's the difference."

I had fewer physical problems than when I was younger, because I'd conquered them through homeopathy. So time went on, and I had no feeling about aging. I was working with younger people, mainly men, and I felt equal to them. Can I possibly be over sixty? I used to wonder, because these guys are complaining over their forties and I really don't feel old.

In 1965 Seema and Jack bought a Volkswagen camper, and after she retired in 1970 they began to travel, visiting friends in Washington and Oregon. They continued an old habit of going off on brief impromptu vacations, looking at the map to find a road that led nowhere and finding a cabin to rent, or, now that they had the van, camping. Jack always took his typewriter with him and he would peck away while Seema went off exploring, paddling in a nearby stream or picking berries for their lunch. They took their dog with them, and left the cats at home. Jack was the driver—Seema had never gotten a driver's license.

Once, Tama took her out for a practice drive.

I was driving down a narrow street, Avocado Street maybe, going about ten miles an hour. I steered into a tree to avoid a car coming toward me— I remember just drifting into the tree. I didn't have a learner's permit, so with horrible presence of mind I jumped out of the car and dragged Tama into the driver's seat before anyone arrived. When they came Tama said she didn't know why she had done it—there was no big damage, but after that I didn't want to get my license.

In their late sixties Jack and Seema became adopted grandparents. Between the sixties and the eighties, the United States opened its doors to professionals from the Philippines, and in 1973 Frolin and Federico De La Cruz arrived in Los Angeles with three suitcases, three small children, and a debt for their passage. When, after a few years, they had saved enough money for the down payment on a house, they moved in next door to the Weatherwaxes. The children gravitated to Seema and Jack, who welcomed them easily into their house and their lives.

They were playing on the porch; they'd gotten used to seeing us around and we looked like grandparents, the door was open and they came in and out of the house. One day they asked, "Would you be our grandma and grandpa?"

From then on the two families formed close ties that continued after the De La Cruz family moved thirty miles away, into the Valley. Seema and Jack attended all their neighbors' parties and celebrations, all the graduations, weddings, and births over the years.

Each year when a new school term started, Seema insisted on hosting a family dinner to mark the occasion. She would bake a whole salmon, or roast a turkey, and there would be mashed potatoes, generous salads, and bowls of fruit, often from their own trees. A large peach tree from Dodie's time gave white peaches in abundance, and when Seema and Jack moved in they planted a fig tree and a kumquat tree, which supplied the whole neighborhood with fruit in season.

When the De La Cruz family moved, they asked Seema and Jack to take part in blessing their new house. Uncertain of their role, the Weatherwaxes walked behind the Catholic priest as he swung his censer and intoned a blessing. They had been given holy water to sprinkle, and they did so dutifully, trying not to choke in the clouds of fragrant smoke. They took their role as adoptive grandparents very seriously.

Soon after Jack and I got married, we thought it would be good to have children. But because of the abortion doctor I went to when I was young, I wasn't able to give birth. So we filled our lives with other people's children. When we lived on Commonwealth Avenue there were a lot of kids whose parents worked on the weekends, so practically every Saturday and Sunday we used to take them to the beach or the park. To this day I have all kinds of godchildren and adopted grandchildren and great-grandchildren.

Old age came suddenly upon Reva, who had stayed active and vital into her nineties. Her second husband, Sam, had died in 1954. In 1965, after eleven years of living alone, Reva married Leon Lerner, an old family friend who then moved in to her back apartment on Edgemont Street. Reva was seventy-nine and Leon was eighty when they married. They lived happily together for about twelve years, until his health began to fail and he became forgetful and demanding. He died in 1979 at the age of ninety-four and his last two years were difficult.

Mother was getting very tired. She had emphysema, and she also had gall bladder problems for about forty years. She was very active in spite of these problems, but it was all catching up with her.

Seema also began to tire under the strain of being responsible for three ill people in her house and she wondered if she would survive her mother. In 1979, the year Leon died, Seema slipped and fell, dislocating her right shoulder. Although she went regularly to a physical therapist and did her exercises, she never regained full motion in that arm. Jack was already ill, and the next year Reva collapsed.

One day she was all dressed up and somebody was going to pick her up to go to a concert or a luncheon when she fell down with a stroke. That was late in 1980, and she died a year and a half later, in May 1982. She was ninety-six.

Freda was also sick, but she was not talking about it. She couldn't help much. When Mother got sick, then Tama used to come very often.

In telling the story of her mother's death Seema's voice dropped low and tears slid down her cheek. She sat quietly, remembering.

Seema's chronic bronchitis had once again deepened into pneumonia. She was in bed with a high fever, hallucinating. By now Reva required twenty-four hour nursing care—Freda and Tama were helping to pay the costs. One night when Jack was out Seema heard a crash in the apartment next door and she went to investigate. Reva lay on the bathroom floor. Seema helped her mother up, hoping not to infect her, and called the nurse, who was asleep and had not heard Reva fall, to help get her back in bed. A week later Reva was much worse and the doctor called an ambulance. They carried the tiny, frail woman on a stretcher through Seema's apartment to the front door.

I stood there as she passed by and I felt, What is she thinking that I don't go with her to the hospital? I didn't dare bend down and kiss her, I could hardly say anything. She was conscious and she looked at me with her brown eyes—she still had those beautiful eyes—and I thought, What is she thinking? How can I tell her I have pneumonia, because she'll grieve for me then? So I never said anything, and I never had a chance to say anything after, because she died.

This is one of the things, as you can see, I still feel very strongly. It's one of the regrets that I have—I would hate to think that Mother died thinking I didn't care about her.

Jack was suffering from pains in his side that his doctor said were due to an infection. Because of the medication he took for his heart, his skin was extremely sensitive—any touch was almost unbearable. He and Seema had talked for years of leaving Los Angeles for a healthier, quieter place, but they hadn't wanted to leave Reva. Now their neighborhood was run down, with "adult" movie houses and drug dealers—where once Seema had walked at night to visit friends on Commonwealth she no longer felt safe in broad daylight waiting for a bus. Also, the climate had changed—it was colder in winter, hotter in the summers and smog hung like a thick yellow curtain over the city. Edgemont Street had been widened, and a lot of the shade trees were gone.

Tama was living in Santa Cruz. Aurel died of a heart attack in 1958, and a year later Tama met and was courted by Max Smith, Superintendent of Schools in Santa Cruz, a red-haired man with a fiery temper. They married in December 1959. Max's death in 1978 brought an end to Tama's third and least happy marriage, and she stayed on alone in the house on Monterey Bay.

Reva and Tama each married three times. Tama was deeply in love with her first husband, Al, and she also loved Aurel, her second husband. No one would ever take Avram's place in Reva's heart. At the end, Reva and Tama, even though they maintained close friendships and family ties, were essentially alone with their memories, looking back on eight decades of married life, each one a widow three times.

Whenever they visited Tama, Seema and Jack spoke of moving up to Santa Cruz where the climate was better and they could be part of a progressive community. They had not felt free to move while Reva was alive, but even after her death they postponed the decision.

Jack didn't want to talk about death; he didn't want to talk about losing faculties or anything like that. No matter how sick he was, even when he was in a bathrobe, he was still functioning. People still kept coming all the time, talking politics.

So I couldn't say, "Hey, Jack, we're getting old, let's do something about it."

If I could have said, which many times I wanted to, "Jack, we both have worked very hard, let's relax, let's do something that isn't so tense," it might have been better for us. Maybe we'd reach a conclusion about how necessary it was to spend more leisure time together, just enjoying each other's company, without thinking all the time, this should be published, this should be written. A lot of energy went into that and a lot of time, and I felt that I could not break into that thing he had to do, because it was most important to him.

I would have liked to spend more time with him, just doing nothing. This was what I wanted to do when we came to Santa Cruz.

All those years ago in Tahiti, Seema had not been ready to spend her life with Clarence "just doing nothing." Now she understood the value of quiet, empty time together with her partner. But Jack was not ready.

It took them two years after Reva died before they wound up their affairs in Los Angeles and sold the house on Edgemont Street. Meanwhile, on April 22, 1984, Ansel Adams died. Jack and Seema and Freda and Frank drove to Santa Cruz so that Seema could go to Ansel's memorial in Carmel.

It was very traumatic. I knew he was not well, but I wasn't prepared for his death.

They had stayed in touch over the years, and whenever she went to visit Tama she also visited the Adamses at their home in the Carmel Highlands, perched high over the ocean.

I had seen him about three or four months before. He had a pacemaker; he had gout; his hands were crippled with arthritis, so it was very difficult for him to do darkroom work any more. He couldn't hold his camera properly, so I knew he was quite sick. But you don't get accustomed to people dying when they're very vital.

The last time I saw him he was writing his autobiography. He'd just bought a big computer, a monster. He took me right away into the computer room and he was playing with it like a toy, telling me, "This goes here and that goes there, and then you press this . . ."

I said, "Ansel, I can't follow that. You're talking Greek! No way!"

"No, you'll understand, I'll tell you!"

Because it was so much fun for him, he was sure that I would grasp it immediately in one easy lesson, and it was one of the most complicated computers. So that was Ansel.

Then Seema's older sister Freda died of stomach cancer.

Freda knew that she had about a year to live, and she never told anybody about it. She didn't want us to know because she didn't want us to grieve or to feel sorry for her. But I could see she was dying.

I always felt sorry that Freda did not live a full life. With all the things I went through, I had a very rich life. Tama had a rich life. Freda didn't have much richness in her life. She was the richest one of us financially, but that was it.

ceLeBRatInG Jack

In December 1984, Seema and Jack moved to Santa Cruz. Hattie and other friends helped them to pack, and they left most of their files and books with friends in Los Angeles, expecting to return later to take what they needed.

figure 49. Farewell party at Edgemont Street,
December 1984. Courtesy of Seema Weatherwax.

A couple of days before we left Los Angeles, our friends gave us a
farewell party. About thirty-four people turned up—we didn't know they
were coming and Jack was in his bathrobe, because by this time he wasn't
feeling very well.

In Santa Cruz, ill as he was, Jack took pleasure in their small garden
apartment on Felix Street. He and Seema walked to the side of the
stream out back and watched the ducks, appreciating the quiet and
beauty of the place. They were there together about a week, then, at the
bank, where he was about to sign papers giving Seema power of attorney over their finances, Jack collapsed with severe pains and had to go

home to bed. A week later he was admitted to the hospital, dying five days later of pancreatic cancer.

In the space of two and a half years Seema lost her mother, her older sister, and Ansel. Now Jack was gone, and she was alone with her grief in a new place.

She lost twenty pounds and most of her hair, and she had trouble making herself get up and get dressed in the morning.

It was hard when I went out and came back and no one was there. I had to keep going—there was so much to do—but my body felt the shock that I couldn't let my mind feel. I didn't want anybody to stay with me. I did a lot of moaning in my bed at night, not crying, but moaning.

After the immediate trauma of Jack's death, Seema's first thought was to organize a memorial for him in Los Angeles.

I didn't want it to be just the sort of thing where everybody gets up and says, Oh, yes, he was such a nice guy, I knew him at such and such a time. I decided that the best way was to show what he was by his own words. I started looking through the papers that we had brought, which was only a handful of the things he had written . . . the rest of it was in the files in Los Angeles. I didn't have a lot, but I thought I had enough to make a showing.

Six weeks after Jack died I went to Los Angeles and I started to look for a place. I remembered this lovely Buddhist temple on Sunset Boulevard. It was like a little oasis, white buildings with gardens. I asked them if they would rent me the place for the occasion. They never had done that before, but they said they would.

Seema's years of organizing experience stood her in good stead as she set about creating the sort of memorial that would best represent Jack Weatherwax.

We had the hall and I made the script, and then I had to call people. I think almost 150 people came, from all over, people of every color, race, and religion. Four friends read passages from Jack's work—I made it like a little performance.

Afterward, the temple people came to me and said, "Thank you for having it here."

Something You Wanted
by John Weatherwax

If you had something you wanted to do, something more important than anything you ever wanted,

If this thing represented for you happiness, fulfilment, the very pinnacle of achievement,

Would it be to have flowers on every table of the world every day?

Would it be to hear and to speak nothing but truth at all times and in all places?

Would it be to abolish death?

Perhaps for you it would be to fill the air and fill the hearts of all people with music, joyous dancing music, sublime music, past, present, future music stirring every being hearing it,

Or, would it be to feed the hungry, to heal the sick, to replace despair with hope?

Would it be that you discovered and set in motion a process by which war were ended?

Would this be something you would want to do?

figure 50. Seema receiving Woman of the Year award,
Sacramento, 1999. Courtesy of Seema Weatherwax.

5

1985–2000: a New Life

Living aLone

WHEN I fiRST CAME HERE, THE fiRST YEAR, I DIDN'T TAKE PART VERY MUCH in the life of the city. I was going through probate, getting my stuff out of storage, unpacking boxes—it was a hectic year.

First of all, I had to get things in order. I didn't just drift into a new life—I thought very seriously about what I wanted to do. I no longer had the responsibility of sick people in my house, but I did have the responsibility of boxes on boxes on boxes.

I looked at all the things that Jack had wanted to finish. I had always been like that—when things were very bad I refused to sit back—I picked myself up and changed things around.

After a year of mourning and introspection, a year of nights spent sobbing without tears and waking to the fresh pain of realizing that she was alone, of days spent sorting out financial and legal problems, paying medical bills and getting herself settled in her Felix Street apartment, Seema decided it was time to enter into community life. She felt secure financially. After her years of skilled work she had a substantial check coming from Social Security each month and proceeds from the sale of the Edgemont Street house in the bank. With care, she could live on her income, and she was used to being careful with money—she had taken over the household finances after Jack had his first heart attack in 1965.

She had been meeting people through Tama and on her own, and now she started to attend cultural and political events in Santa Cruz.

I went to everything by myself most of the time—I wanted to decide for myself, and I didn't want to be pushed into anything.

She was invited to join a progressive discussion group that met twice a month in someone's house, reminding her of the groups she and Jack had hosted. When she heard about a strike in a local cannery, she organized a benefit at Tama's house.

Do you know the first thing I did after I came here? I had an art sale. I had two portfolios of Taller de Gráfica Popular from Mexico—one I kept intact and the other I sold separately, and the money went to the cannery workers.

Once Seema had met local people it was an easy step to her next event. She organized an exhibit at a local community center of her diverse collection of prints and artwork. Seema provided refreshments for the opening reception in the usual lavish style of her family, and the exhibit was well-attended. Her public life in Santa Cruz had begun.

Soon after her exhibit she contributed artwork to an exhibit of Hispanic art at the University of California, Santa Cruz. She had begun to accumulate a new circle of friends, while keeping ties with old friends and family. Her carefully maintained file of telephone numbers and addresses was expanding.

Chan Weston, who lived about an hour away, started driving over several times a month to visit her; Charis Wilson, who was living in Santa Cruz with her daughter, heard that Seema was nearby and the two women renewed their old friendship, finding an intimacy they had not known in the old days when each was absorbed in a demanding relationship. When Charis was preparing her memoir of her years with Edward Weston, Seema contributed photographs, and they reflected together on their decisions to leave the men they had loved so much.

seema and me

Her voice on my answering machine was resonant and rich-toned, crackling with age and vitality. She spoke precisely, with a trace of a Yorkshire accent: "My name is Seema Weatherwax."

figure 51. Rose, Sara, Margie, Hattie, Seema in foreground,
Yosemite, 1987. Courtesy of Seema Weatherwax.

I replayed the tape several times to make sure I had heard it right.

"I attended your film screening last night at the Women's International League," she said, "and I want to tell you that your film on El Salvador is excellent. I know something about photography, and I think you did a very good job."

How nice of her, I thought.

The voice continued, "However, in your film about aging, I found something lacking. I am eighty years old, and I know something about that subject. I would like to talk to you about it. Please call me back."

I screwed up my courage to return her call. My documentary on aging had won a big award—that meant a lot to me, a single mother living with my teenage son, making films that earned very little money. I was anxious and curious about an older woman's criticism of the film. At forty-three I hadn't noticed my shift toward middle age. Seema at eighty seemed old to me.

She invited me to discuss my film over tea with a group of her friends. She lived across town at Cypress Point on Felix Street, a complex of garden apartments in a quiet enclave of trees, grass, and winding paths. On my way from the parking area a mother duck followed by her little ones crossed my path, waddling down to the nearby creek.

When I rang the bell at apartment 5 a very short, elderly white woman opened the door and smiled at me. She wore slacks and a patterned sweater, and her voice was throaty, softer in person than on the phone. "You must be Sara. I am Seema and I'm so glad to see you. Come in, come in."

Six other women sat in the living room of the small apartment, on a carved wooden couch softened with tapestried cushions and on chairs upholstered in a fabric of faded rose. Framed black-and-white photographs, oil paintings, and woodcuts hung side by side along each wall, at eye level, as they would be in a museum or gallery. A black doll and a Russian doll sat together in a child's chair.

Seema poured tea from a flowered china teapot, and we passed around plates of poppy seed cake. I sat balancing my gilt-trimmed cup and saucer on my knee, feeling nervous, like a student coming up before an examination board. But this group of women in their sixties and seventies spoke in quiet, warm tones, and as we chatted together I relaxed.

Seema began, "I was very impressed with the quality of all your films, but the one on aging made me feel hopeless. When I went home that night I stayed awake for a long time, trying to sort out my feelings. No one in the film looked happy or excited about what they were doing. I thought, there must be some way other than this business of waiting to die." She looked around the room. "What do others think?"

One woman said in a kind, hesitant voice that she had felt a little depressed after watching the film, and another woman agreed.

"After I saw your movie," she said, "I went home and cried. I said to myself, 'Is this what I have to look forward to?'"

"The movie was well made," Seema said, "and it showed life as it is. However, when you show war, you don't show only the horrors—you need to give people hope."

It was the best critique I'd been offered. They helped me to realize what was missing in my film, a depiction of a group like this one, elders getting together to carry on their lifelong tradition of activism.

After our tea the others left and Seema gave me a tour of the pictures in her apartment. A photographic mural of a snowy landscape with Yosemite's Half Dome in the background dwarfed everything else in her bedroom. Seema told me she had printed it from a negative taken by Ansel Adams when she worked as his assistant.

In the living room, a snapshot in a small frame on a table showed a young, lithe Seema dancing wildly with a man she identified as Edward Weston.

"That was on a break during the first photographic workshop we had at Yosemite. There's Ansel at the piano, laughing at us cutting up."

Another photo showed Seema setting up her camera and tripod, her feet braced on a granite slope.

A black-and-white portrait of Seema by Edward Weston, emphasizing the strong angles of her face, hung next to a portrait of a handsome young man, Edward's son Chan. Seema told me she had first met Chan in the Film and Photo League in Los Angeles. She said they had been "very close," and that Dorothea Lange had sent her the photo of Chan as a keepsake. I was interested in the love life of this beautiful, talented woman, with her warmth and vivacity, and I was also interested in the Film and Photo League. I had studied their work and wanted to ask many questions, but on this first meeting I just looked and listened.

Some of the photos on the walls were hers: trees rising from the ground like elephant's legs, an aproned farm woman holding up her painting of a rural scene.

I was struck by the clear lines and intent focus of these pictures. "I carried my camera everywhere I went," Seema said. "I always asked people if it was all right for me to take their picture."

Very different in style and subject from the photographs and woodcuts, an oil portrait of a man with kind dark eyes and a long gray beard, wearing a prayer shawl and a *yarmulke*, hung in the small corridor leading to the bedroom. This was Seema's maternal grandfather, Joseph Abelov from Kiev.

"Grandfather was trained as a rabbi," she said, "but in those days rabbis weren't paid a salary, and he wanted to get married and raise a family."

So Seema was Jewish, like me.

A low bookshelf in the hall was filled with small Russian carvings and framed photos. I picked up a double frame that held photos of a younger Seema and a kind-faced man at a desk.

"That was my husband, Jack—he was a writer. He died three weeks after we moved here from Los Angeles. That was a year ago January."

I put my arm around Seema. She took my hand and squeezed it. "It was a terrible time. We had been hoping to have some quiet time here, but we didn't come soon enough."

When we said goodbye, Seema hugged me and said, "Please come back again." Before returning to my busy life, I walked out to the creek and stood on the small wooden bridge looking down at the water. I would return to this peaceful place many times.

Many years later, Seema reminisced with me about our first meeting.

I gathered about seven of us to meet with you, and I thought we had a wonderful discussion. You listened with both ears, and from then on we became friends. We did a lot, including our trip to Yosemite. That meant we were very good friends, because I thought a lot about who would go on that trip with me.

It was my first visit to the famous valley, and the first time I spent extended time with Seema. We'd met for breakfasts and lunches, attended readings and concerts, made latkes at Hanukah, compared matzo ball recipes at Passover, and shared Thanksgiving dinner. Now I would see a significant piece of Seema's past.

When we stopped at the Valley View I stared across at the green and gray vastness, mountains of bare stone rising from the green valley, with waterfalls descending in streaks of silver. I saw light and shadow, a spirit of immensity—I saw the landscape as I had learned to see it from Ansel Adams's photographs.

Seema had invited four of us to accompany her on what would be her last visit to the Valley.

The youngest [Rose] was twenty-six, and then there was one in the middle forties, and I was eighty-two, and then there were two in the middle [Hattie Brown and Margie Katz, both in their sixties]. We wanted to go for about four days, long enough to really enjoy something, and when all of them were able to get away from work, because they were all working women.

I made arrangements to rent two condos, and we decided that the two people from Los Angeles [Hattie and Margie] would drive up in their car and the three of us from here would drive directly there and so it came to pass. There wasn't snow on the ground—it was on one side or the other of Memorial Day. It was still beautiful, the Valley was lush. It was like Yosemite used to be, because we were away from the main tourist traffic. I had the same feeling I had when I used to go there.

Seema was quiet as we drove through the Valley on Sunday morning, quiet as we trooped into the grand old dining room in the Ahwahnee Hotel and ordered our breakfasts. She resumed her cheerful banter once Hattie and I decided to compete over who could eat the most bacon, and by the time we left to visit the old studio complex, she was fully in charge.

We went to Ansel Adams's studio, and I was able to show where the darkroom had been. It was no longer being used every day, only when they had a camera workshop. I could still point to the apartment I used to live in, which was on the same hill, but it was very different. The studio, when we came there this time, was nothing whatsoever like it used to be. It used to be a very beautiful place. You went in there and it was very serene. It was not a commercial shop like it is now.

A blue-green bowl flirted with me from a shelf in the studio gift shop. I picked it up, admiring its fineness, its watery glaze made by a local potter with copper from the river rocks. When I went up to pay for my bowl, Seema was talking to the manager, telling him she once ran the darkroom, in the days when all that was sold in the shop were Ansel's photographs, film, and some very good cameras. The young man stood there politely, glancing from time to time over Seema's head to survey the flow of business under his charge.

I saw Seema through the manager's eyes, a little old lady in polyester slacks and a sweater like thousands of others who came into his store every day in the busy summer season. I was not yet able to see through Seema's eyes as she remembered the refuge where she had spent four magical years.

After visiting the studio we set off for a hike.

We decided to go to Mirror Lake, and I did some hiking, which I shouldn't have. I felt that I was in pretty good shape physically, even at eighty-one.

So we started out on the trail, and it wasn't used very much, obviously. There were a lot of pebbles and it was not easy walking. It was about two miles. I made it there and we enjoyed the lake, and then we came back on the same trail.

That night I had a charley horse that you can't believe. It hurt so badly, I had to crawl on my hands and knees on the floor to go to the bathroom. I'd had charley horses before after too much hiking, but after five minutes of exercise they would go away. Nothing would make this go away—it was absolutely excruciating pain. Fortunately Margie had a homeopathic remedy with her, arnica. It took about two hours before the pain went away.

I said to myself, from now on, you can't do what you used to do when you were younger. So that was a lesson I learned, a very painful lesson.

I remember comparing my vitality with Seema's, wondering how well I would adjust to physical limitations in my own old age.

Later she gave me a Polaroid snapshot of our group, taken just before the hike (fig. 51). As I look at the picture nearly two decades later, Seema in the center beams, looking vibrant. I am struck by the sight of my younger self in shorts, with tanned legs and hair not yet touched by gray. The tall trees tower over us, a reminder that age and time are relative.

Returning to Santa Cruz from Yosemite, Seema continued to build her new life. She went on working with the Women's International League for Peace and Freedom and the National Association for the Advancement of Colored People, eventually becoming a member of the board for each organization and working to bring the two communities together. She told her white friends in WILPF that it was not enough to invite African Americans to join them—they would have to ask how they could help with events and issues that were important to the black community. A few of the women from WILPF were willing to try.

We were asked to help with the NAACP banquets, so for three years we made the salads. We had to have quantities of salad for a hundred and fifty people, you know, and so we did.

I was still the only person, at first, who had any real connections with the black community. I used to go to some of the church functions, so then they asked me to come to social events. But the others were still not taking part.

Some of the WILPF women would say, "I'm not racist."

They didn't understand. I don't think people are racist if they haven't learned how to work together. Racism involves something much deeper than that. But, they didn't feel at home. This is the basic thing.

Somebody said, "I don't know how to talk to them."

I said, "They have children, they have work, they have school, they have to buy groceries, they have to do the laundry, don't you have to do the same? What do you talk about to your other friends? We have the same needs. So talk about our mutual needs, and then you find out the differences have not got that much meaning."

After a while they were working with the people, not at the people, if you know what I'm saying. Now that I don't do as much, I feel happy because other, younger people are there, doing the same thing as I have done through the years. And it's good.

I've always seen my political work as building connections instead of tearing down oppressive systems.

When Rabbi Litvak called to invite NAACP members to a Passover seder, Seema and Reverend Renfrew from the Baptist church represented the black community and helped organize the event along with the rabbi and a member of the temple. Seema chuckled at the idea that she could represent the black community, adding that she helped edit the *Haggadah*, the text written for the seder.

I understood what the Jewish community would find distasteful and what the black Baptist community would understand, so I made corrections.

For a number of years the Jewish–African American seder, with its emphasis on freedom and justice, was a high point of the progressive calendar in Santa Cruz.

In her late eighties Seema moved from Felix Street to a slightly smaller but similar garden apartment in La Posada, a senior housing co-op on the other side of town. I had left Santa Cruz, encouraged by Seema to trust a new relationship. My husband and I lived in Portland, Oregon. When I first visited Seema in her co-op apartment, I was at first put off by the institutional entrance and reception area. I walked apprehensively down a wide corridor lined with identical doors, but when I knocked at Seema's door and she welcomed me into her living room with its sliding glass doors opening onto a garden courtyard, with her familiar furniture and pictures on the walls, I felt reassured.

Seema had enlisted a friend to help her arrange her furniture in the new living room just as it had been at Felix Street, which helped as her eyesight grew dim. Determined not to allow herself to stagnate, she kept changing the art on the walls, even when she could no longer see it well—she said she didn't want her frequent visitors to be bored.

She had become a well-known figure in Santa Cruz and there was a constant stream of visitors to her apartment. Over the years, as I saw Seema walking more and more carefully from her apartment to check her mail, calling out greetings to neighbors and staff, I realized the value of the reception desk, the smooth-tiled corridors, and the wide paved entrance.

Around 1990 she bought an answering machine to keep track of her many callers, and an electronic reader so that she could read postcards and notes and pay her own bills. Watching her as she sat at the table that held her reader, twiddling knobs to adjust focus and brightness, arranging her reading material on the platform and moving it as she read the magnified text on the screen, I saw the same competence that had led Ansel Adams to proclaim Seema the best of all his master printers.

In the early 1990s, I interviewed Seema for my book about women's appearance, *Look at My Ugly Face!* She spoke thoughtfully about how her standards of beauty had changed and were still changing, even now, influenced in part by her conversations with me. She'd recently decided to let her hair grow out into a curly bush after years of having it cut "short, with a bit of a curl . . . like twenty other women I know. I got tired of being institutionalized by my hair!" Her vivid face with deep-set, dark eyes surrounded by a shock of white hair reminded me of Albert Einstein.

When my book was published Seema helped me to set up a reading in Santa Cruz. The bookstore was crammed with some of my old friends and many of Seema's in attendance. Seema spoke briefly, emphasizing my discussion of racism and racist standards of appearance, encouraging the audience to read the book and make up their own minds about the subject.

She continued to seek out friendships with creative people of all ages and backgrounds, and she spoke at schools and libraries, encouraging young people to think independently and take chances in expressing themselves. She was delighted by an invitation to speak to the children of migrant workers in Bakersfield, where she had photographed the farmworkers' camp so long ago.

When she could no longer go outside alone, because of shortness of breath, she arranged for friends to come and pick her up for outings. She made the best of her increasing physical limitations and seldom complained, but from a few comments she made, I could tell that her independent spirit felt confined.

I miss going outdoors, to the countryside. It doesn't work out with the friends that I have, because, you know, everybody's busy and we have just so much time, so we get together over a cup of tea or over something to eat. But I've been dying to go to a lupine field—just being able to walk with the lupines and pick them, that sort of thing. And I miss going to the ocean, when you just sit there and see a little hint of the waves.

REMEMBERING, TELLING

The small theater in downtown Santa Cruz was bursting at the seams. I made my way through the crowd to Seema, who was sitting in the front row, resplendent with a huge corsage pinned to her sweater. She had lost weight since the last time I'd seen her; her face was more sharply defined, and her hair was longer, standing out from her scalp in a fine white aureole. This was her first time out of her apartment in five

FIGURE 52. Seema after Robeson concert with Harriet and Alex Bagwell, Santa Cruz, 1998. Photo by Sara Halprin. Courtesy of Sara Halprin.

weeks. She was not going to miss the concert she had dreamed of and planned for, the concert honoring Paul Robeson's centennial that brought her back from the brink of death at ninety-two.

In late December, Seema's chronic bronchitis had deepened once again into pneumonia. Her regular homeopathic physician was out of town, and she didn't want to go to the hospital, fearing she would choke to death in a hospital bed. One of her many friends, a young health-care worker, dropped by and realized how ill her old friend was. She took her to a doctor who prescribed antibiotics and an inhaler. Seema's friend ordered her to stay in her reclining chair and keep warm, and she and others took turns coming in.

For three days and nights I sat up in that chair. On New Year's Day we had a meeting scheduled to organize the concert. The others asked if we should cancel, and I said, "No way." So we had a meeting with me sitting here with an inhaler and taking antibiotics, and beginning to breathe again a little bit.

The success of the concert was a testimony to Seema's organizing abilities. She had worked hard over the past twelve years to bridge the deep gulfs between black, white, Jewish, and Hispanic communities in Santa Cruz. As she had done with Jack's memorial, Seema insisted on honoring Paul Robeson through creative performance.

People said, you must have a speaker, and I said no, I must not have a speaker. You're going to hear the story of Paul Robeson through other forms, dance, singing, music, and no speeches. The only speech we had was from one person who spoke less than five minutes about her experience as a kid with Paul Robeson.

At the end of the concert, Seema was given a standing ovation from an audience intent on celebrating her as well as the great African-American singer and activist.

The next day, after brunch at a local restaurant with some of the performers and organizers, Seema and I had some time alone. I was jolted by my friend's account of her illness, and touched by her resolute recovery. "I feel better than I have in years," she said. "It was a clearing for me."

When I first suggested to Seema that I should write a book about her life, I had no idea of the difficulties we would encounter. My choice to work with a living person instead of a fictional character meant that I had to follow her actual path, not the path I might want to create for her, nor the path she might imagine for herself.

The work of remembering and telling her past became Seema's way of understanding her life. She told me she was not introspective—she was not interested in probing deeply into feelings, hers or other people's, but often she produced startling insights born of long observation and patience. Other times it was as if a wall thicker than time separated her from her early experience.

When she responded to some of my questions by saying, "I don't remember," or, "It's not important," I felt frustrated, wanting to understand the stubborn spirit that had repeatedly turned challenge into opportunity. I did not at first understand that her memory was making choices that were meaningful and could help me to go deeper. Noticing what Seema did not remember or what she felt was not important, noticing what she put at the margins of her life, noticing also what was important to her, what she remembered with delight and in vivid detail—this would be the way for me to define her path and what lay on either side of it.

I remembered Seema's recurring dream of going to a social event and being abandoned by friends and family.

Suddenly I looked around, and all my friends were gone. I kept looking, and I realized I had no way to get home. I felt panicky, because everyone left without me.

This dream makes me think of the time my father died—I felt abandoned by him. Later, when my first husband and I were living in Paterson, New Jersey, often he wouldn't come home at night. I didn't know where he was. I was alone in our house, and I was afraid.

The dream offered a pattern for me to understand Seema's life as a whole. She had maintained family ties with cousins and nieces and nephews on the East Coast, in England and in Russia, and she had kept in touch with a wide network of friends from Los Angeles, Yosemite, and Santa Cruz, but death took many of them away. Death also took each of her partners, her father and mother and sister Freda, and finally it took Jack from her—then she had to find her own way home.

Seema's dream could have been my dream. I know her fear of being alone, abandoned by friends and family, having to find my own way, without conventional support, alone with my memories of the dead, alone, finally, with my irreducible self.

Her dream could have been my dream, pushing me toward a separation from ordinary life that shocks and frightens me, toward an independence that in my deepest self I know I need.

Thinking of mortality, hers and mine, I was concerned about the slow process of gathering information and preparing to write. So was Seema.

"I am half-blind and half-deaf and I won't live forever, so I think you had better hurry up and write this book!"

So we began.

Sitting in her blue recliner chair near the sliding glass doors of her living room, Seema told me most of her stories. Here, as she gradually had to limit her excursions outside, she organized her many activities, spending hours on the telephone, visited constantly by friends and family. She set aside time for me, but we were often interrupted by some-one poking a head in to say hello or to drop off an audio tape or a mes-sage. Even so, we found many hours in person and many more hours on the telephone to return to parts of her past, taping the interviews that would become most of the raw material for this book.

Seema's intensely visual orientation was evident in the way her rem-iniscences often began: "I see in my mind's eye . . ."

DOING MORE

In July 1999 I sat on the familiar wooden couch with its tapestry cush-ions, looking through photo albums. Seema had finally found profes-sional help to organize her overflowing boxes—archivist Charles Hanson started working one day a week with her in 1996. A hobbit-like man with an unruly mop of dark hair that he liked to toss out of his eyes

figure 53. Seema with Jason Weston, selecting photographs for show, Santa Cruz, 2000. Courtesy of Seema Weatherwax.

fiɢure 54. Seema with Charles Hanson, Santa Cruz,
ca. 2000. Courtesy of Seema Weatherwax.

with a dramatic gesture, Charles created indexed photo albums chron-
icling the major periods of Seema's life: one album for her childhood in
Russia and England; another for the East Coast years in Boston and
New Jersey; one each for Los Angeles, Tahiti, and Yosemite; and one
album still in progress, for Santa Cruz. Like others who entered Seema's
life as helpers, he became an intimate friend. It was Charles who would
curate Seema's first show of her photographs at the Mulberry Gallery.

As I leafed through the album labeled "Los Angeles," I saw Seema's
life with Jack as a procession of images. She was usually photographed
side by side with Jack, in front of their house on Edgemont Street, with
Jack's sister Clara and her husband Jerry or with their friends Witz and
Joe Biddle, with a group of square dancers, or with her sisters and Reva.
As marriage and adoption extended their family, the gatherings grew
larger and more ethnically diverse and the three Aissen sisters and Reva
were shown surrounded by much taller, younger family members. The

snapshots showed Seema growing stout, wearing glasses, her hair turning gray, then white, while Jack grew a beard and it turned gray and then white; finally he was thin and thinner, and he looked very ill in the last photos taken in Los Angeles.

In the album labeled "Santa Cruz," two newspaper photos caught my eye. In one, taken in 1988 when she was eighty-three, Seema stood near a tree, holding a camera. She looked clear, determined, a kindred spirit to the tree. Her white, curly hair was short, fluffed around her head. The photo was taken for an article profiling her for a Santa Cruz paper, and the caption reads, "Seema today: feeling the itch to do more."

She did a lot more over the next decade. She was active in the community; she arranged for many of her photographs to go to university collections and to the Smithsonian Institution; she did radio and TV interviews about her work with Woody Guthrie in the Dust Bowl camps; she spoke at schools; she kept track of old and new friends and family.

In 1999 she was named Woman of the Year by the California State Assembly, which led to another news article. In the accompanying photo she looked up and off to her left. Her face had aged considerably since the last photo—her nose was more pronounced, her wrinkles deeper, her eyes, still dark and striking, were sunken, and her long hair stood out around her face in an untamed cloud of white.

I noticed on this visit that Seema had become physically frail. In the years I'd known her she had shrunk several inches in height. She said her bones had settled—she could feel it in her swollen ankles. When she came to the door to hug me on my arrival, the top of her head came to my breastbone, and when I put my arms around her, I could feel the bony curve of her back. Her smile was as warm as ever, her attention clear and focused. My old friend glowed even as her bones sank.

One of the recurring threads in our conversations, ever since we first started exchanging confidences, was sex. I have had close friendships with several women who lived well into their nineties, but none except Seema ever discussed sex openly with me. Although some of her confidences were strictly off the record, she was frank about her sexual feelings as she grew old.

I have not been with any sexual partner since 1979. In '79, when Jack had to have the pacemaker, and they started him on heavy medication, things really changed. Even though we didn't lose our desire for each other, it was not possible to have sex—we had to be satisfied with embraces and kisses.

After Jack died I would have liked to have a sexual partner, and a loving companion. There was one married friend whom I was attracted to, and if things had been different with Chan I might have wanted to pick up with him again.

When I came to Santa Cruz Chan was already not well, but we were very good friends, and we used to, like, date. He'd pick me up, we'd have breakfast or lunch together. Very soon after I came here, we hugged each other and it was like a shot of electricity. I immediately shut it off, because I knew that it would not be a good thing to do anything. He felt warmly toward me, but he was in a relationship which had lasted for a few years with a younger woman, a very nice person—I did not want to break up her life. Chan had not changed his point of view about multiple relationships, and I was definitely not into that. Also, there was a question of AIDS.

I have men and women friends, and I like to hug a woman but that's all I ever want to do is hug, but with a man there's a kind of a thrill attached to it. I haven't stopped having sexual feelings, and they're not as strong as they were maybe five years ago, but they're still there. It's like someone who loves to drive a fast sports car. You may no longer be able to drive the sports car, but that doesn't mean you don't want to do it.

Seema decided to put her apparently inexhaustible energy into printing some of her old negatives.

She and Jason Weston met and became friends shortly before Chan died. When Seema mentioned to Jason her wish to do more printing, he invited her to visit his darkroom, where she spent a long day working with him on some of her old negatives.

By fall of 2000, as Seema's opening at the Mulberry Gallery drew near, I noticed in our telephone conversations how much stronger Seema's voice was. She was printing regularly with Jason and working with Charles to plan the show. She was happiest and most well when she felt herself in control, making decisions about her photographs that other people helped her to implement. When she felt that others were taking over, then she started to feel tired. This theme of control was a central motif of her experience of aging.

I like to hold someone's hand when I walk, lightly, not too tight. I still need to have control.

When I walked with Seema, I felt the touch of her dry, papery skin as we held hands, like schoolgirls in Leeds, walking into a field blue with wildflowers to pick a bouquet for the table at home.

epilogue

"So that's it?"

"That's it."

"It doesn't seem like much of an ending."

I had just finished reading the first whole draft of my manuscript to Seema. It took four days, with her sitting in her recliner and me sitting opposite her, as close as possible, reading in my clearest voice. We had agreed that I would read about twenty pages at a time, and whenever she heard something she wanted to question or discuss, she would raise her hand and I would mark it. After twenty pages I'd go back over the marked passages.

The reading had gone well, with fewer objections than I'd expected, mostly helpful corrections, and a couple of spirited arguments. Anything that was a direct quote from Seema was up for change—I figured she had a right to revise her own voice. My opinions and historical research were another matter. We had some disagreements (she hated the adjective "stout" and preferred "heavy," which I thought didn't describe her at all; she objected to every use of "Bolshevik," most of which I didn't mind dropping), but what I had not anticipated was to see Seema with closed eyes, deep in reverie, occasionally nodding, smiling, or frowning. I realized that she was reliving her life as I read.

She was relieved to know that I hadn't exposed her most vulnerable secrets or named names she preferred not to use, relieved that I had presented her life in a way that felt authentic to her.

I had wrestled, as any biographer of a living subject must, with these questions of veracity versus intrusion. Not having anticipated the strength of Seema's insistence that I omit some of the stories she had told me, I once complained that I was struggling to know how to write about her. She responded tersely: "Just write the facts. You can embellish it later."

There were two issues at stake. Seema had already declared that some of the facts she had given me were confidential, not to be disclosed. She also felt that there was no need to probe deeply into sensitive issues. Following her wishes, I could simply have written, for example, that she ended her relationship with Clarence and went on to another, more passionate relationship with Chan Weston, who then introduced her to his father, Edward Weston, and that it was Edward who introduced her to Ansel Adams. These were facts with which Seema was comfortable, but the bare outline of facts lacked the human interest that drew me to write about Seema in the first place. Her stories of her struggles and low points, her mistakes and regrets as well as her triumphs drew me close to her, made her story vivid and made me reflect on my own issues. Leaving out these stories would impoverish my portrait of Seema as a complex woman facing problems with no easy resolutions.

On the other hand, there were facts about her political and romantic affiliations that she absolutely refused permission to include. I respected her decision, reluctantly at first, and discovered that the key to writing was not held in any single fact but rather in the pattern of the whole life, discovered by exploring feelings as well as facts in detail.

Our biggest dispute was about her relationship to the Communist Party.

When I asked Seema to be specific, she reiterated her belief in communist philosophy and refused to be pinned down about whether or when she and Jack were Party members, saying, "It's not important," or "I don't remember."

At first I was puzzled. Was it her memory, fogged by the years and the many issues and conflicts, the complicated ins and outs of progressive politics; was it that she was unwilling to compromise her many friendships by admitting something she felt would not be well-received? I argued with her—"Seema, the Communist Party is not a threat anymore—no one will be upset with you," but she was adamant.

"It will stop my meaningful discussion about things that are necessary. I don't want to hurt anyone, so there has to be omission on some levels."

I wanted to know more than she was willing to discuss, why she continued to support the Party long after it was clear to many that the Communist experiment in the Soviet Union was a dismal, terrible failure.

"You had those disagreements, but you were free, here, to have them."

"I wasn't free to say I was a Communist. We could not say we were Communists for many, many years."

The ending disappointed her. I wasn't sure what she had hoped for. A summing up perhaps? A definitive statement of what her life had meant? She said later that she wished I had written more about her last years, especially about all the things she had done to bring the Jewish and Black communities of Santa Cruz together.

I thought about the time, after her show, when I accompanied her to an NAACP meeting at which she presented a check to the president. The check represented a third of Seema's profits from the sale of her photographs, not a large sum, but a large gesture from a woman living on limited means. I saw at that meeting that Seema was held in high esteem by the membership, as people took pains to speak slowly and clearly so that she could hear them, and came up one by one to hug her and say in warm tones how glad they were to see her there.

Once we had finished reading the manuscript, I told Seema I would leave the next day after breakfast. Early in the morning, before I was really awake, while I was fumbling to pack my suitcase, Seema stood before me in her white nightshirt, barelegged, tilting her face up toward mine as if she could see my eyes, but I knew she could not. She seldom slept more than five hours in a night, and when I visited her, sleeping in a rollaway bed in the living room of her one-bedroom apartment, she patiently accommodated my need to sleep longer.

This morning she had lain in bed awake, waiting to talk to me about revisions. I had written that she still hoped in her mid-nineties to have a love affair and she had flagged that passage. We'd agreed that I would change the wording, but we hadn't yet found a phrasing that satisfied both of us. Now she was saying earnestly, "Don't write 'love affair.' Relationship is the word I keep coming back to. It's so much more than an affair, not just sex but affection, intimacy. I don't want people here thinking I'm looking for sex with them—I get enough proposals!"

I realized how alive she was, immersed in her life, nowhere near ready to be written off with a neat phrase.

On September 12, 2001, Seema's niece Joy and her husband Frank drove up to Santa Cruz from Los Angeles. Joy had wanted to give Seema a belated ninety-sixth birthday party, as she'd been out of the country on Seema's actual birthday in August. Now they debated about whether to cancel the party in the sad aftermath of the September 11 attack on New York.

"We decided that in times like these people need to be together," Seema told me when I phoned her. "So we had an open house. Twenty-one people came."

"Seema, where did you put them all?" I was incredulous, knowing the size of her apartment.

"We just opened the sliding doors and moved the plants to one side of the patio. Tama sat out in the sun in a comfortable chair, and people came in and out."

Of course. The loneliness of many of her elder friends was well-known to Seema, even though her own life was packed with people and events. At a time of national mourning, why not combine a wake with a birthday party? People do need to be together.

The change in the American political climate since 2001 has given me a different perspective and new respect for Seema's caution about revealing details of her political affiliations.

Her first photography show was not the last. In 2002 Seema and Jason had a show together as part of Santa Cruz's Open Studios, and hundreds of people passed through the small studio. They had another successful show in 2003.

In June 2004, Tama died peacefully in her bed, surrounded by family and friends. Blind and unwell by the mid-1990s, she had left her house on the bay at Seema's urging and moved into a sunny apartment on the third floor of La Posada where I often visited her while staying with Seema. Tama had a gentle humor and kindness that endeared her to me.

In her last years Tama couldn't come down without help, and Seema, who disliked elevators, seldom went up, so the two sisters spoke on the phone twice daily, sending food and audio tapes up and down by means of friends and helpers. Each had her own friends and her independent life, but they stayed in close connection for ninety-seven years.

A month later, Seema told me she still expected to hear from Tama each day, after breakfast and after dinner. I wondered how much longer I would be able to share stories and laughter with Seema.

How could I possibly sum up Seema's life, when the things I remember most vividly are so small? But those small things conjure up larger ideas. Her yearning for independence, her genius for intimacy, her clear-sighted awareness of her issues in extreme old age, along with her passion for justice, are qualities I treasure in her. A dear stubborn woman who never undervalued the impact of her own small personal voice, she has lived her life intensely, influencing those around her to value each moment, to believe in ourselves, to risk the hazards and joys of intimate relationship, and to see the world around us through a lens of wonder.

Portland, Oregon, October, 2004

sources and acknowledgments

My primary sources have been interviews and conversations, supple-
mented by written and visual materials. As this book has emerged from
the rich personal context of Seema's ever-expanding circle and also
mine, so my discussion of sources blends into acknowledgments.

Seema Weatherwax has been my original, invaluable source of
memory and opinion about her own life and the events in which she
took part. After an initial interview with Seema, videotaped in 1987, and
a second interview with her, audiotaped in 1995 for a research project
on aging, I began taping interviews for this book in May 1999 and continued on a regular basis, at least once or twice a month, through
December 2000, then taped four more interviews in 2001. Seema and I
also had many informal discussions by telephone and in person
throughout the entire period, and I kept notes of these in my journal.

In many instances we revisited the same material several times, as
Seema would reflect on her memories between interviews, or as I had
further questions. I compared transcripts of different accounts of the
same events before compiling my narrative, then revised these accounts
according to continuing input from other sources, which I then
checked back with Seema.

I also had access to tapes and transcripts of interviews with Seema's
mother, Reva Lerner, conducted by her granddaughter Joy Gonzalez in
1976 and by her son-in-law Jack Weatherwax in 1979. Hearing Reva's
sweet, clear, Yiddish-accented voice with her emphatic way of speaking

gave me a vivid sense of her and her role in the life of her family. I interviewed Joy Gonzalez in Los Angeles in 2000; we had several subsequent exchanges by phone and e-mail.

I interviewed Seema's sister, Tama Smith, twice in 1999, followed by a number of informal discussions in person and by phone. Tama, always a loyal younger sister, insisted that any discrepancies between her memory of shared events and Seema's should be resolved in Seema's favor, because, she said, "This is her book."

Seema's close friend Hattie Brown, who became a friend of mine over the years, helped in every way she could.

Jack's nephew, John Weatherwax, and his wife Lita opened their home in Florence, Oregon, to me, offering memories, photos, and a genealogy of the Weatherwax family.

In Santa Cruz Marge Frantz helped me to understand the historical context of many of Seema's stories and pointed me to other people and books; Charles Hanson, whose archival work with Seema's papers and photographs has been invaluable, helped again and again to track down photos, clippings, memories, and all sorts of miscellaneous and precious bits; the late Jane Podesta, Rita Bottoms, Elena Feder, Myra Barnes, Frolin De La Cruz and her daughter Fides Ebow, and other friends shared memories with me. The staff at La Posada were unfailingly hospitable and helpful. Oneil Canon invited me to his home in Los Angeles and spoke to me at length about his association with Seema and Jack. Members of NAACP and WILPF in Santa Cruz welcomed me and helped in many ways.

Jason Weston gave me a detailed account of his work with Seema as he developed her old negatives and prepared for her show. He was generous in giving technical advice on photography for the text, and he has been a source of joy and comfort through the long process of selecting and preparing photos for this book.

WRITING

After the initial accumulation of interviews with Seema, Tama, and Reva, I searched for a narrative voice and structure to organize and present the mass of material I had at hand. Then came the task of filling in and revising areas where neither my knowledge nor Seema's memory were sufficient. These were not linear processes; they developed in relationship to each other. For example, Seema's decision to print her old negatives was made after we had been working together for several months, so the narrative structure that begins and ends her story with the account of her first show was not conceivable at the outset of my project.

My first tentative attempts to tell Seema's story were read supportively and critically by my writing group in Portland, "Ursula's Urchins," which emerged from a master's writing class at Portland State University, offered in spring of 1999 by Ursula K. LeGuin. Ursula suggested that I write a straightforward biography and reassured me that I would eventually find my voice to do so, and the Urchins patiently read draft after revised draft. The Center for Excellence in Writing at PSU generously provided space for our meetings. My thanks to Ursula, also to Kamala Bremer, Marj Casswell, Patrick Cummings, Gerri Hayes, and Eric Stumbaugh, and especially Susan Russell, who read along with the other Urchins, then helped me with the final version.

Marge du Mond read the manuscript at an early stage and gave impeccable advice. Willa Schneberg brought her finely honed sense of intensity of language to bear on the framework of the narrative, also helping in the final revision.

Elizabeth Hadas read the completed manuscript and gave encouraging feedback several years before it became possible for her to take it on as a project for the University of New Mexico Press. As my editor at the Press, she has managed to combine friendship, support, and a piercingly intelligent perspective with patience and humor.

PHOTOGRAPHS

Most of Seema's collection of photographs and art is now housed at Special Collections, University Library, University of California, Santa Cruz. I'm grateful for the help of Christine Bunting, director of Special Collections, and Don Harris, at the UCSC photography department, for providing a copy of Edward Weston's photo of Seema. Eventually Seema's albums and remaining personal collection will also go to UCSC.

Seema also donated photographs to Special Collections at the Stanford University Library. Her collection of photographs of the 1933 earthquake in Los Angeles is there, also some photographs of the Hollywood Strike of 1945, most of Seema's vintage prints of Woody Guthrie and the Shafter Farm Labor camp, some vintage prints of the photographs Seema took during her trip to Mt. Lyell with Ansel Adams, and publicity photographs Seema took of the calypso singer Sir Lancelot.

Ansel Adams' photograph of Half Dome, printed by Seema, is now at the Santa Barbara Museum of Art.

In 1988 Seema donated Jack's papers documenting his collaborations with Diego Rivera and Frida Kahlo. These are listed as the John Weatherwax Papers, 1928–1988, Archives of American Art, Smithsonian Institution.

Dorothea Lange sent Seema a print and the negative of her photo of Chan Weston as a gift, and Seema gave the negative to Jason Weston, who kindly provided a print for this book. Ann Adams Helms sent Seema the photograph which appears in this book of her parents, Ansel and Virginia, with Seema in front of Best's Studio in Yosemite. Jason Weston supplied prints for his photograph of Seema in 2000 and for his photo of Seema with me in 2004.

All the remaining photographs in the book were supplied by Seema Weatherwax, and copied, scanned, or printed from original negatives by Jason Weston.

PUBLISHING

In league with the expert and kindly editorial guidance of Elizabeth Hadas, mentioned above, Maya Allen-Gallegos, managing editor at University of New Mexico Press, has been courteous and responsive, shepherding me through the mysteries of preparing a manuscript with photographs for publication. Melissa Tandysh was a delight to work with and I love her design of the book and cover. David Farber, co-editor of the CounterCulture series at UNM Press, offered helpful suggestions for rewriting the manuscript and did so with grace and generosity.

personal support

I've had strong support for my writing from Arny and Amy Mindell, whose groundbreaking development of the theory and practice of process-oriented psychology, or process work, has provided a background for my understanding of just about everything.

Noah Martineau, Amy and Kevin Tye, Toby Long, Cher Sauer, other family, friends, and students have encouraged me throughout the years of working on this project. They and my grandson, Dylan Tye, remind me why and for whom I write.

Herb Long, my husband and partner, has listened, counseled, loved, and supported me always.

bibLiOgRaphy

Complete citations are listed alphabetically at the end of this section.

peRsONaL hIstORy, ORaL hIstORy, aND bIOgRaphy

The historian whose work has been most evocative and influential for me is Gerda Lerner, and her book *Why History Matters* offers a complex and courageous response to her question, why was it that she, a Jewish refugee from Nazi Austria, "spent over thirty years documenting and studying the history of American women and of black women and never thought of studying the history of Jewish women" (Lerner, xiii). Working through her issues of internalized anti-Semitism as well as her keen sense of gender inequity and racial injustice, she concludes, in a way that Seema would approve, "we must learn and learn very quickly to . . . celebrate difference and banish hatred" (Lerner, 17).

Because my book crosses the line between oral history and biography in several respects, it has been helpful to read and discuss issues pertaining to oral history as well as to biography.

Selma Leydesdorff, Luisa Passerini, and Paul Thompson's "Gender and Memory," Luisa Passerini's, "Memory and Totalitarianism," and especially Alessandro Portelli's *The Death of Luigi Trastulli and Other Stories* have been helpful in supporting my understanding of the value of psychology in oral history, exactly the sort of psychology I practice myself as a process worker, noticing and appreciating the significance of glitches and lapses in memory, of diversity in differing accounts of the same events, of the human aspects of history.

I am grateful to Sandy Polishuk for discussions of her process in writing and compiling her oral history *Sticking to the Union* as well as for her reading of my manuscript at an early stage.

Bell and Yalom's *Interpreting Women's Lives* and the Personal Narrative Group's *Revealing Lives,* two feminist texts, helped validate my sense of the importance of context and relationship in women's lives.

Elinor Langer's biography of Josephine Herbst was an inspiration to me, setting an example of thorough research and insightful writing about her subject, and I am grateful for her discussions and encouragement in the early days of my research.

RUSSIa

Anna Reid's *Borderland,* John Maynard's *Russia in Flux*, Harold Shukman's *Russian Revolution*, and Adam Ulam's *The Bolsheviks* offered valuable background material on the first part of Seema's life. Leo Rosten's *Joys of Yiddish* was my guide to the intricacies of spelling and understanding the Yiddish references sprinkled throughout Seema's anecdotes.

HISTORY aND CULTURE Of THE aMERICAN Left

For an understanding of radical politics in the U.S. at the time of Seema's first political involvement, I read the text that swayed her to join the Young Communist League, Marx's *Value, Price and Profit*, also the anthology *Highlights of a Fighting History*, and Peggy Dennis's *Autobiography of an American Communist.*

Other sources that helped me to understand the longer term picture of left-wing politics and culture in the U.S. include: *The Encyclopedia of the American Left,* Malcolm Cowley's *Dream of the Golden Mountain*, Michael Denning's *The Cultural Front,* Maurice Isserman's *Which Side Were You On?*, Howard Zinn's *People's History of the United States,* and the irreverent and informative account of her own experience by Jessica Mitford, *A Fine Old Conflict.* The anthology *Red Diapers* offers firsthand accounts of people raised in radical American families, parented by people of Seema's generation, as does Kim Chernin's story of her mother, Rose Chernin, Seema's good friend and comrade.

Norman Klein's *History of Forgetting* helped me to imagine the Los Angeles of an earlier period.

For information on the cultural aspects of the Popular Front, I turned first to Tom Waugh's *"Show Us Life,"* with several articles which provide background to the work of the Film and Photo League, also to Russell Campbell's *CinemaStrikes Back.*

Marshall Berman's review of Studs Terkel's *Working* gave a clear, succinct picture of the Popular Front as it was seen by the Left.

Studs Terkel's oral histories of working America, especially *Hard Times, The Good War, Working*, and *Race*, provide context and perspective to many of Seema's memories.

Clara Weatherwax's novel *Marching, Marching* shows the lyric spirit of leftist idealism and exemplifies the Weatherwax family spirit.

From Jack's many pamphlets and papers, I found his pamphlet "The African Contribution" to be an excellent example of his dedicated, pioneering documentation of African-American culture.

Deborah White's *Too Heavy A Load* and Anne Scott's article "Most Invisible of All" gave helpful background for Jack and Seema's work with the National Association of Colored Women.

PHOTOGRAPHY

I have included in the following list a selection of books, many of them recommended by Seema, that helped me to gain a sense of historical context and a beginning understanding of the immense achievements in photography made by the circle of friends Seema knew so well during her years in Yosemite and long after. Of these, Jonathan Spaulding's biography of Ansel Adams and Charis Weston's account of her years with Edward Weston were especially useful.

citations

Alinder, M. S. and A. G. Stillman, Eds. 1988. *Ansel Adams, Letters and Images 1916–1984*. Boston, Little, Brown.

Bart, P., Ed. 1979. *Highlights of a Fighting History: 60 Years of the Communist Party, USA*. New York, International Publishers.

Bell, S. G. and M. Yalom, Eds. 1990. *Revealing Lives: Autobiography, Biography, and Gender*. Albany, New York, State University of New York Press.

Berman, M. 1974. Working. *New York Times Book Review*. New York.

Buhle, M. J., P. Buhle, et al., Eds. 1992. *Encyclopedia of the American Left*. Urbana, IL, University of Illinois Press.

Buhle, P. and E. B. Sullivan, Eds. 1998. *Images of American Radicalism*. Hanover, MA, The Christopher Publishing House.

Campbell, R. 1982. *Cinema Strikes Back: Radical Cinema in the United States, 1930–1942*. Ann Arbor, UMI Research Press.

Chernin, K. 1994 (1983). *In My Mother's House*. New York, Harper Perennial.

Cowley, M. 1980. *The Dream of the Golden Mountains: Remembering the 1930s*. New York, Viking Press.

Cunningham, I. 1970. *Imogen Cunningham: Photographs*. Seattle, University of Washington Press.

Davenport, A. 1999 (1992 Focal Press). *The History of Photography: An Overview*. Albuquerque, University of New Mexico Press.

Denning, M. 1996. *The Cultural Front: The Laboring of American Culture in the Twentieth Century*. New York, Verso.

Dennis, P. 1977. *Autobiography of an American Communist: A Personal View of a Political Life 1925–1975*. Westport/Berkeley, Lawrence Hill & Co.

Enyeart, J., Ed. 1989. *Decade by Decade: Twentieth Century American Photography*. Boston, Bulfinch Press: Little, Brown and Co and Center for Creative Photography, University of Arizona.

Glauber, C. 1997. *The Witch of Kodakery: The Photography of Myra Albert Wiggins, 1869–1956*. Pullman, WA, Washington State University.

Hirsch, R. 2000. *Seizing the Light, A History of Photography*. Boston, McGraw-Hill.

Isserman, M. 1993. *Which Side Were You On? The American Communist Party during the Second World War*. Urbana, IL, University of Illinois Press.

Kaplan, J. and L. Shapiro, Eds. 1998. *Red Diapers: Growing Up in the Communist Left*. Urbana and Chicago, University of Illinois Press.

Klein, N. M. 1997. *The History of Forgetting: Los Angeles and the Erasure of Memory*. New York, Verso.

Langer, E. 1984. *Josephine Herbst: The Story She Could Never Tell*. New York, Little, Brown and Co.

Lerner, G. 1997. *Why History Matters: Life and Thought*. New York, Oxford University Press.

Leydesdorff, S., L. Passerini, et al., Eds. 1996. *Gender and Memory*. International Yearbook of Oral History and Life Stories. New York, Oxford University Press.

Lorenz, R. 1998. *Imogen Cunningham: On the Body*. Boston, Little, Brown, Bulfinch Press.

Maddow, B. 1989. *Edward Weston, His Life*. New York, Aperture.

Mann, M. 1970. *Imogen Cunningham, Photographs*. Seattle, University of Washington Press.

Marx, K. 1935 (1865). *Value, Price and Profit*. New York, International Publishers.

Maynard, J. 1962. *Russia in Flux: Before October*. New York, Collier Books.

Mitford, J. 1977. *A Fine Old Conflict*. New York, Alfred A. Knopf.

Palmquist, P. E., Ed. 1995. *Camera Fiends & Kodak Girls II*. New York, Midmarch Arts Press.

Partridge, E. 1998. *Restless Spirit: The Life and Work of Dorothea Lange*. New York, Viking.

Passerini, L., Ed. 1992. *Memory and Totalitarianism*. International Yearbook of Oral History and Life Stories. New York, Oxford University Press.

Personal Narratives Group, Ed. 1989. *Interpreting Women's Lives: Feminist Theory and Personal Narratives.* Bloomington, Indiana, Indiana University Press.

Polishuk, S. 2003. *Sticking to the Union: An Oral History of the Life and Times of Julia Ruuttila.* New York, Palgrave Macmillan.

Portelli, A. 1991. *The Death of Luigi Trastulli and Other Stories: Form and Meaning in Oral History.* New York, State University of New York Press.

Reid, A. 1997. *Borderland: A Journey Through the History of Ukraine.* Boulder, CO, Westview Press.

Rosten, L. 1968. *The Joys of Yiddish.* New York, McGraw-Hill.

Scott, A. F. 1990. "Most Invisible of all. Black women's voluntary associations." *Journal of Southern History* 56: 3–22.

Shukman, H., Ed. 1988. *The Blackwell Encyclopedia of the Russian Revolution.* New York, Basil Blackwell.

Spaulding, J. 1995. *Ansel Adams and the American Landscape: A Biography.* Berkeley, University of California Press.

Stillman, A. G., Ed. 1977. *Ansel Adams California.* Boston, Little, Brown and Company.

Terkel, S. 1970. *Hard Times: An Oral History of the Great Depression.* New York, Pantheon books.

———. 1974. *Working: People Talk About What They Do All Day and How They Feel About What They Do.* New York, Pantheon Books.

———. 1984. *The Good War: An Oral History of World War II.* New York, Pantheon Press.

———. 1993 (1992). *Race: How Blacks and Whites Think and Feel About the American Obsession.* New York, Anchor Books.

Ulam, A. B. 1965. *The Bolsheviks: The Intellectual, Personal and Political History of the Triumph of Communism in Russia.* New York, Macmillan.

Watkins, T. H. 1993. *The Great Depression: America in the 1930s.* Boston, MA, Back Bay Books (Little, Brown and Company).

Waugh, T., Ed. 1984. *"Show Us Life": Towards a History and Aesthetics of the Committed Documentary.* Metuchen, NJ, The Scarecrow Press.

Weatherwax, C. 1935 (reprinted, facsimile ed. in 1990 by Omni). *Marching! Marching!* New York, John Day.

Weatherwax, J. M. 1964. *The African Contribution, Part II.* Los Angeles, The John Henry and Mary Louisa Dunn Bryant Foundation.

White, D. G. 1999. *Too Heavy a Load: Black Women in Defense of Themselves, 1894–1994.* New York, W.W. Norton.

Wilson, C. and W. Madar. 1998. *Through Another Lens: My Years with Edward Weston.* New York, North Point Press, Farrar, Straus and Giroux.

Zinn, H. 1995. *A People's History of the United States: 1492–Present.* New York, Harper Perennial.

Libraries

In Portland, the Multnomah County Public Library has been a constant resource for books, microfilm, interlibrary loan, and help in tracking copyrights.

In Los Angeles, Oneil Canon provided access to the Paul Robeson Center collection of Jack Weatherwax's papers and books.

Thanks to Sarah Cooper and Patricia Martinez at the Southern California Library of Social Research for lugging out their bound copies of the *People's World* along with boxes of ephemeral material from the fifties through the eighties in Los Angeles.

Thanks also to the Tamiment Institute at New York University, for information on the history of American radicalism and oral history.

The Internet has been a resource center for many aspects of this book. Here is a selected list of sites, with posting dates as available followed by retrieval dates, that I found especially helpful in supplementing Seema's memories of her past:

"Desna is the River of My Childhood," Valentin Shkolny. 1998. June 19, 1999. http://www.chernigov.us/History/desna/index_e.shtml.

"Chernigov: Early Communal History; The 20th Century; The Holocaust Period and After." Encyclopedia Judaica. 1972. Jerusalem. Keter Publishing. Museum of Tolerance Online Multimedia Learning

Center. The Simon Wiesenthal Center. 1997. June 19, 1999.
http://motlc.wiesenthal.com/pages/t013/t01398.html.

"Roundhay Park." Leeds City Council. May 28, 1997. August 11,
1999. http://www.leeds.gov.uk/tourinfo/attract/parks/roundhay.html.

"The Red Cars of Los Angeles," Los Angeles, Past, Present and
Future, University of Southern California Archives. January 15, 2002.
http://www.usc.edu/isd/archives/la/historic/redcars/.

"A California Water History." March 21, 2000.
http://are.berkely.edu/courses/ENVECON162/cawaterhist.html.

"Photo-League: New York in the 1930's and 40's." March 27, 2000.
http://www.telefonica.es/fat/ephotoleague.html.
http://www.telefonica.es/fat/ephotoleague.html

"World War Two in Europe Timeline." The History Page. August
11, 2000.
http://www.historyplace.com/WorldWar2/timeline/ww2time.htm.

"Awaiting His Return, Charles White." Narratives of African
American Art and Identity. March 30, 2000.
http://www.inform.umd.edu/EdRes/Colleges/ARHU/Depts/ArtGal/.
WWW/exhibit/98–99/driskell/exhibition/sec3/whit_c_01.htm.

INDEX

figure 55. Seema and Sara, by Jason Weston, Santa Cruz, ca. 2004